Where is my Home?

a Hungarian refugee in England and Holland

GEORGE POGANY

First published in 2014
by CreateSpace

1st edition 1.0

Text copyright © George Pogány 2014

George Pogány has asserted his right to be identified as the author
of this work

All rights reserved. No part of this publication may be reproduced, stored
in a retrieval system or transmitted in any form or by any means without
the prior written permission of the publisher nor be otherwise circulated
in any form of binding or cover other than that in which it is published and
without a similar condition being imposed on the subsequent purchaser

ISBN 978-1-4973937-7-6

to Roy and Fre, our true friends

Table of contents

xii Introduction

9 In England

35 The first eight years

67 Getting a DPhil.

93 The last years in England

107 Moving to Holland

137 Delft

147 Amsterdam

165 Training managers

183 Visiting Hungary

207 Epilogue

In this house with starry dome,
Floored with gemlike plain and seas,
Shall I never feel at home,
Never wholly be at ease?

> from *World Strangeness*
> Sir William Watson (1858-1935)

Introduction.

I was born in Hungary and escaped to England with my wife and four-year-old son after the revolution of 1956. *When Even the Poets were Silent*, a book about my experiences as a Jew in Hungary under fascism and communism, was published in January 2012. I was extremely lucky to escape the death camps and end up instead in a labour camp in Vienna. After returning to Hungary I studied chemistry and worked in nationalized industry under communist rule. This present volume continues my autobiography, describing our lives as refugees in England and then, as expatriates, in Holland. I also describe life in Shell as I experienced it when working for this company for almost thirty years. I also wrote a previous book, *How to be Happy in Holland*, published in 1995. It is long out of print and I have taken the liberty to repeat some of the observations I made in it. This is a true story, but a few names have been changed. I apologize for the occasional scientific discussion, but I am a scientist and while I tried to keep these discussions short and simple I couldn't leave them out.

I am indebted to Emeritus Prof. Dudley Jackson and Prof. Robert Fine for their help and encouragement. I am also grateful to Liam D'Arcy-Brown for correcting my English and advising me on the structure of the book.

1

In England

SO THIS IS England, the land of Shakespeare, Newton and Darwin. Together with my wife Vera and four-year-old son István, we had managed to escape communist Hungary. The main motivation for us had been to secure a better and safer future for István. What would become of him? Would he be another scientist like his father, grandfather and uncle? Would he become a true English gentleman, a member of the Church of England? Would he marry a nice English girl and produce a few English grandchildren? Would he study at Oxford as I had hoped? These were my thoughts as I watched the fast moving clouds in the refugee camp at Hednesford. We had already spent two months in refugee camps in Austria, and now I was up early to explore this latest, English camp.

The camp commandant was an Englishman who spoke no Hungarian, and to my great surprise the interpreter at the camp was someone I knew—Imre, an engineer who used to work as a lecturer at the technical university in Budapest. His wife, Terike, was a former colleague of mine. By the age of 22 she had been a graduate mechanical engineer and mother of three children, two of them twins. She was the second wife of Imre, who had another child from his first marriage. In Hungary we had sometimes gone on company outings together. I liked Terike—beautiful, intelligent, and always cheerful—but I didn't like Imre, who was always showing off and acting in a superior manner. Imre felt it necessary to explain to me that he had come to England alone, simply to prepare the ground, and was planning to go back later for his family. I found this explanation, or rather excuse, strange. I thought he shouldn't have left Austria, as it would be much more difficult to carry out his plan from England, if indeed it was his plan. More to the point,

WHERE IS MY HOME?

he should have never left without his family. Of course he never did go back. He emigrated to the US, divorced Terike, and married again, in all likelihood producing yet more children. His style didn't change in the camp, where, amongst other duties, he had to recruit helpers from amongst the refugees to work at managing the camp. One of the requirement was that the candidates should be able to speak some English. His own English was very good, and his standard question was always asked over the telephone: 'Can you spell your name?' Speaking a foreign language on the telephone is always difficult, and spelling in English is quite different from spelling in Hungarian.

Our pocket-money in the camp was £1, 10/- a week, much more than we had got from the Red Cross in Austria. Vera and I both found jobs in the camp. She was conveniently employed by the camp nursery, and I became a storeman. We were each paid £2, 10/- a week, and our employment cards were stamped. We felt really rich.

A canteen ticket for Hednesford Refugee Reception Centre

In England

We were free to come and go as we pleased, and were amazed by the abundance and cheapness of everything. An Indian tradesman came to the camp selling shirts for 10/- apiece. In Hungary I had had to save for two months before I could buy one shirt. One Hungarian refugee went to the nearest town, Cannock, and returned driving an old English taxi which he had bought for £10. It was, of course, dilapidated, and belched copious amounts of black smoke. He had no idea about the cost of maintenance, insurance, and road tax, or of the need for a driving licence! I too made an important purchase—a Woolworth's screwdriver with a red, wooden handle. I still have it, and it is still in perfect condition, in spite of the fact that I used it as a universal tool, tin opener, and so forth. 'Made in Sheffield' is engraved on it.

Food in the camp was adequate, but a little strange. We were served fine, white bread with the soup, but they took the bread away after the soup was finished. Hungarians eat no bread with their soup, but do eat a lot of bread with the main dish, even if it is pasta- or potato-based. There was almost a second Hungarian Revolution until this cultural difference was realised and remedied. Meeting Colman's Mustard for the first time was also an experience I shall not forget. The mustard was in a wooden container on the table. I had no idea what it was, but wanted to investigate. As I touched its smooth, shiny surface, my finger went right through it, and I licked the mustard off. Never again!

I had a diploma in chemistry from the University of Budapest and six years of industrial experience, but I was afraid that this would not be accepted in England and so I had left it behind with all my other official papers. I was prepared to do any menial job at a laboratory, if necessary, and hoped to progress given time. Vera's uncle, Feri, who lived in London and was also a chemist, translated my CV, which I learned by heart. It started: 'I am an industrial chemist of twenty-nine...' Armed with this, I went from the camp to London, to the Labour Exchange, which had a special register for scientists. I had to change trains at Crewe, and when the train stopped I found myself searching everywhere for the handle to open the door, but there was none. Who ever heard of a door without a handle, and a railway coach door at that? I banged on it in desperation: 'Help! I want to get out!' Eventually someone opened it for me and explained that the way to open the door from the inside was to lower the window, reach out, and open it from the outside. The handle was on the outside by way of a safety feature, so that children couldn't accidentally open the door while the train was moving. It was quite different to the trains in Hungary.

The Scientific Register at the Labour Exchange sent my details to a number of chemical companies. Fortunately, at this time there was hardly any unemployment in England and I got several invitations for interviews. I had learned some English at school, but my knowledge was very poor. I could read a text and translate it with the help of a dictionary, but I couldn't find a Hungarian–English dictionary anywhere and only had a German–English pocket dictionary. I was hopeless in understanding spoken English, especially if spoken with an accent. Every time I became stuck for words, I started to recite my CV from the start: 'I am an industrial chemist of twenty-nine...' People usually recognised my problem and stopped me quite quickly.

I tweaked my CV to suit each particular application. It would be unkind to call this lying; I simply emphasized different parts of my career. If for instance they had asked for a laboratory assistant, I wrote that I was an experienced laboratory chemist. This was, of course, true; I simply neglected to mention that this represented only one year of

In England

my entire experience. If they asked for a design engineer, I proudly highlighted my many years of experience in design.

My first appointment was with the Chemical Supply Company in London. They didn't ask many questions and offered me a job on the spot as a chemist at a salary of £650. They also paid my travel expenses, which came in useful. Of course I accepted the offer without even thinking about it. It did a lot to improve my morale, and I started to adjust my mental picture of my future life in England. Washing dishes had been ruled out of. We were rich. We had made it.

Within a few days I had got another interview, this time from Lever Brothers. For some reason which they never told me, they decided that I was not the person they were looking for and paid my expenses and gave me a box of soap. This was a bit of a set-back, but I had after all already accepted one job offer. You can't win them all, I thought. The third interview was with Schweppes. They were looking for a laboratory chemist, and when I told them I had only one year's experience as an analytical chemist, they got somewhat angry.

'But you've written that you have several years' experience.'

'True, several years, but as an industrial chemist, not as an analyst.'

They searched for my letter so as to confront me with it, but fortunately they couldn't find it. They didn't even give me a bottle of their bitter lemon, just paid my expenses and sent me on my way.

That same afternoon I had another interview with A. Boak & Roberts, a firm of engineering contractors. The vacancy was for a job much like the one I had been doing in Hungary, and they asked me a few detailed questions. This time I didn't start quoting my CV from the start, and managed to say more. In response to a question about distillation column designs I uttered the name of Foster Wheeler, a well-known American equipment manufacturer. Then I draw them a diagram showing how we used to calculate the necessary height of the distillation column. They instantly recognised it, but said that there was now a more modern method. By the end of the day I had an offer from them with a salary of £900. I omitted to tell them that my expenses were already paid, so they paid me as well. After returning to the camp, I wrote to the Chemical Supply Company to tell them that I was not going to work for them after all.

I also went to the Horstman Gear Company in Bath. It was a wasted journey, but the factory belonged to the family of Mrs Eastwood, the same English lady, Joyce Horstman, who before the war had supported my wife as a child through the Save the Children fund. After a pleasant reception we quickly agreed that they had no job suitable for me. Fortunately, they too paid my expenses.

There was one more interview, at Shell in London. The manager of the personnel department didn't ask many questions and put up with my boasting about my experience of working in a petroleum refinery in Hungary. A little while before, Shell had bought a factory making ammonium nitrate fertilizer, and I was happy to say that I had designed just such a plant. I also waved at him the letter from A. Boak & Roberts, adding that I needed a quick response, otherwise I would go to work for them, but for some reason (!) he didn't even want to read it.

'The vacancy is in our Carrington works, at Manchester,' he said, 'and first you will have to go there for an interview. If they accept you, your salary will be £950, and a rise to £1,000 has been already agreed.'

'I have very little time…,' I protested.

'Go back to the camp and tomorrow you'll find our letter

In England

of invitation in the post.'

And indeed the next day I received a letter inviting me to Manchester for an interview. They also enclosed a first-class return railway ticket, which soon became the talk of the camp. A refugee getting a first-class ticket! What's more, on arrival at the station a company limousine with a driver was waiting for me. My relatives in London were also pleased to hear about this offer: 'Nine-hundred-and-fifty pounds in Manchester is worth £1,200 in London. And getting a job at Shell, you'll have a job for life,' they said. They were right on the first point, but wrong on the second. By the time I had received my badge for twenty-five years of service, job security had disappeared even at Shell.

At the factory three people interviewed me, and I was surprised how much emphasis they put on being sure to get my own preferences. For that salary I would have been willing to clean the toilet! Eventually they offered me a job in the Economics and Scheduling department, but before I could start I needed a work permit. I was told to return to the camp and wait. Getting the work permit was a simple administrative step, but in order to get it I needed a job. This became a kind of chicken-and-egg game while I waited patiently for any word from Shell, which never came. Finally I decided to take matters into my own hands, and on the 8th of April I travelled up to Manchester and reported for work. The work permit was granted by the local authorities the same day.

Shell found me a room as a lodger with the family of Mr and Mrs Brown, who had two sons, aged twelve and thirteen, and a daughter of ten. I had a room and board and a very friendly welcome from the whole family. Mrs Brown served good, hearty meals, and I still remember the first time I got a large piece of sea-fish, which I never saw in landlocked

WHERE IS MY HOME?

Hungary. Fifty years later, my wife and I still keep in contact with their daughter.

While I was starting my new job, Vera and István travelled to Broadstone in Dorset at the invitation of the Eastwoods, where a friend of theirs, Cicely, a retired teacher, gave them accommodation for a few weeks. She was a typical spinster, tall and slim and very much set in her ways. Vera learned a lot from her about British etiquette and table manners. She was a devoted member of the congregational church where Jack Eastwood was a minister. It was very emotional for Vera to meet the Eastwoods, who waited for her at the station with a bunch of yellow roses, after so many years of correspondence only. Joyce Eastwood came from a wealthy family, who owned a factory making gearboxes. Joyce had been brought up strictly while Queen Victoria was on the throne, and later than was usual had married Jack, a man

With the Eastwoods (the author on the right, Vera at the rear)

In England

a few years her junior, who came from a simple family in the North of England. Their kindness knew no bounds, they were both excellent hosts, and their door was always open to guests both invited and uninvited. Later, when they retired and lived almost in poverty, we occasionally helped them.

Vera and István stayed for three weeks in Cicely's house, which was quite close to the sea with a small port for fishing boats. At the ebb tide, people collected cockles on the beach, and my wife and son tasted them for the first time. In the meantime I had managed to rent a furnished house in Davyhulme, some five miles west of Manchester. I had heard about this house from the Browns, and I walked there to look at it but nobody answered the door. I rang the bell next door, where the Griffiths family lived (to be precise, it was then only Roy and his wife Free, a young couple, recently married, whose children were born later). Roy worked in a building society, and eventually worked his way up to become one of its directors. If there are stereotypes, he was that of a true English gentleman. He had impeccable manners, polite and always helpful. Free was an attractive lady, very slim with dark blond hair and blue eyes, and nobody could laugh more heartily than she could. Roy opened the door, and after a little difficulty understood my problem and promised to talk to the owner. To begin with the owner wanted to sell the house, but Roy persuaded him to let it to us furnished. Then the owner wanted three months' rent in advance, which was simply impossible for us. So yet again Roy intervened on our behalf and one month's rent was agreed on. With our accommodation arranged, I collected my family from Broadstone during the Easter holiday and I too met Cicely and the Eastwoods for the first time.

WHERE IS MY HOME?

Our rented house and its furnishings were in a rather neglected state, but it was a lot better than a refugee camp. In place of a garden there was a miniature jungle. So before I went to Broadstone to collect my family I placed on the mantelpiece a card bearing the words 'Remember Traiskirchen', to remind Vera, every time she might be inclined to complain, that we had had it far worse in that camp in Austria.

On Easter Monday we returned all three of us together to our new home and settled in for the night. According to one Hungarian superstition, we counted the number of corners in the room we slept in for the first night, so that our dreams would come true. I don't remember what, if anything, I dreamt, but it must have been a pleasant one. That first morning, we sat down to have breakfast—buttered bread, and coffee—it was a bright, sunny day, the birds were providing a concert, and we felt on top of the world.

'We made it,' we concluded. 'Our son has a real chance to assimilate, he'll become a real Englishman, and won't experience the pain of persecution.' At the time I was not yet sure of the difference between integration and assimilation, and even today the Oxford Dictionary provides little help. My own definition today, decades later, would go like this: integration is behaving like the locals and being accepted by them as an acceptable foreigner; assimilation is not only behaving, but also *feeling* like the locals, and being accepted as one of them. We were sure that we would merely be able to integrate, since we were too old to assimilate, but that István might in time feel more English than Hungarian.

After breakfast I had to catch a bus to work. The fare was 7d, and it was a real struggle to work out how much change I should receive if I paid the conductor with half a crown. In Britain's pre-decimal currency, half a crown

In England

was 2/6d, and 1/- was worth 12d, so the correct change was 1/11d. I remember how, when I came home that day, István, without looking, ran straight across the busy street to greet me and I was so shocked at his lack of care that I smacked his bottom. Even now, it still hurts me to think about how I spoilt his joy at seeing me and made the meeting painful for him. If only I could turn the clock back.

Soon after we'd settled in, we invited Roy and Free for dinner. We asked them to bring some cutlery and a chair, because we didn't have enough for all of us. In Hungary the greatest delicacy was what in England is called 'Chicken Maryland'—pieces of chicken covered with egg and breadcrumbs and deep fried. We decided to prepare this dish for our guests, and Vera bought the largest chicken she could find; unfortunately it was an old fowl intended for soup only, totally unsuitable for the purpose. The meat was uncooked and tough, with blood still visible around the bones. Our guests did their best to eat what they could and

The Griffiths

praised the cook as well, but it was a struggle. The conversation too was limited to the few words we knew, but we supplemented it with body language. In spite of all this we remained friends throughout the years and we still visit each other occasionally.

Not understanding English was very disturbing. Opposite our house were a few shops, and on Saturdays the locals used to meet in front of them. I stood nearby and listened, trying to understand some of the conversation, but it was total gibberish to me. Looking at the people conversing and occasionally laughing, their faces expressing peace and harmony, I thought 'I shall never be part of this community.' Fortunately I was wrong.

I had learnt English at school and had a very limited vocabulary, but the biggest problem was the pronunciation. There is no 'w' in the Hungarian language, and pronouncing this and the 'th' sound has been a great problem to us. An additional problem we faced was that most people spoke with a strong Mancunian accent. When I wanted to buy three wooden stakes for the garden and asked for the price, the shopkeeper said 'threepny.' 'How much?' I asked again, and he repeated the sum three times, but I still couldn't understand it. Finally he wrote it down on a piece of paper and I understood that he had been saying 'three halfpennies.' This was very strange to me, first of all because Hungary did not have a coin that was half of another coin, and, even if we had, we would never have expressed the sum in this way! 'Why couldn't you say one and a half pennies?' I thought.

The English language uses many more words than Hungarian, and you can see this by the size of an English-Hungarian dictionary compared to the smaller Hungarian-English ones. In Hungarian we have, for example, a word for 'elephant' (*elefánt*) and one for 'bone' (*csont*), but no

In England

specific word for 'ivory': we simply say *elefántcsont*. The extra words in English allow the speaker to use more nuances, but a foreigner can't always appreciate the differences. The fact that English people use little or no body language was an extra barrier to communication. It took a long time to appreciate the different meanings of the same words pronounced with different emphasis. The ending of a sentence with 'isn't it?' or 'do you?' or such like was very strange to me. Once, I wanted simply to say 'dog', but the listener didn't understand it, so eventually I had to bark! And then there were the colloquialisms we had to learn. When after a sentence someone said to me 'you can say that again!' I actually repeated what I'd said. And why did somebody suggest that I was trying to pull his leg, when I hadn't even touched it?

We gradually learned the language from Joyce, an old spinster living with her even older mother, whom we met in the church. Joyce was a professional teacher, by now retired, and came to our house to teach us colloquial English. Her only reward was a packet of Woodbine cigarettes. Slowly I became able to understand people talking to me face to face, but talking on the telephone was still impossible. So my boss asked for an extra telephone to be installed parallel to his, and I had to listen in to all of his conversations. In turn, he listened in to mine, to make sure nothing went wrong. And there were spelling problems, too: one Friday afternoon I had to go home, but my boss was not in the office. I wrote a note—'Have a nice weak end' and put it on his desk…

Another problem was that we didn't know any everyday English proverbs or nursery rhymes and couldn't help our son with the sounds that animals make. Children learn these things at home, and we couldn't find any references to them in our simple dictionary. Why was the rabbit called

WHERE IS MY HOME?

'Brer'? Who was Alice? And Winnie the Pooh?

Aside from our problems with this strange language, we also had to get used to strange food. For a start, we were overwhelmed with the choice in the shops, and especially by the fact that fruit and vegetables were available out of season. But the cooked food was very different from what we were used to, starting with those 'thick soups' and continuing with that same, unappetising, brown-coloured sauce called 'gravy' poured on almost everything. The gravy in Hungary is always red, from the paprika powder. English coffee tasted like warm water, and tea had to be mixed with milk to be drinkable. The milk had to be added to the cup *before* the tea was poured. We used to eat beans in Hungary, but never in a tomato sauce. We quite liked it, but my brother-in-law and his wife were more conservative, and after opening a tin they always washed off the tomato sauce.

Soon after arrival in England

In England

We found the desserts strange, too, but exceptionally good, and loved custard on everything. The real treat, of course, was sherry trifle, with bread and butter pudding coming second. Ketchup was new to us, and István soon got hooked on it. He used it on everything from fried eggs to Christmas turkey. Vera on the other hand got hooked on Marmite, again something we had never had in Hungary. My favourite dishes were steak and kidney pie and blue Stilton cheese. We liked fish and chips, which was still wrapped in newspaper in those days. We used to have it on weekends. We also liked Chinese restaurants, which served tastier food than the conventional English ones.

Eating out while travelling around the beautiful British countryside was far from being a great culinary experience. Small villages, even in tourist areas, had one cafeteria only, with a menu that could be summed up as 'egg and chips, sausage and chips, or egg and sausage and chips, in addition to the almost compulsory baked beans on toast.' Once, while touring Scotland, we were really hungry but could only find a posh, expensive hotel. We decided to push the boat out, but because by now it was three o'clock the kitchen was closed. We had afternoon tea, served beautifully on a silver tray, consisting of tea, one scone per person with butter and jam, and two tiny pieces of cucumber sandwich, good enough to serve as an ornament. The crusts, which we always enjoyed the most, had already been carefully removed.

We also had to get used to the different drinks. In Hungary, people would drink wine, often diluted with soda water, or beer, or a short, strong *pálinka* fruit brandy. Hungarian beer was of the 'lager' type, with lots of froth, always chilled, quite different from English 'bitter'. Nobody in Hungary had a sherry before a meal, and whisky and Coca Cola were not available. And we never even heard of cider, or gin and tonic. We got to like cider as a cheap substitute to beer and wine. It was also strange that in the pub we had to pay for our drinks one by one, as we collected them from the bar. In Hungary we had paid when we left the premises. And the licensing laws were not only strange but downright annoying: during the warmest part of the day, the pubs were closed. In Hungary everybody could buy an alcoholic drink, but in England you had to be at least eighteen years old.

There were some difficulties in coping with the cultural differences as well. Hungarians like to exaggerate, while the English are famous for their understatement. The locals never corrected us, but initially we found them a little cold and emotionless. We found the houses cold, too, especially the bathroom, where there was no heating at all. Our bedroom had just a single bar electric heater. Once, we visited some friends, Geoff and Iris Nichols, on a cold winter evening, and from the outside we saw that their living-room window was open. We debated this, but decided not to say a word to our hosts. But when our hostess complained about the draught and put a mat in front of the door we mentioned the open window. 'I know,' she answered. 'We like the fresh air.'

Like most people, we had a coal-burning open fire in our living room. We had to sit in front of it to get any benefit from the limited heat it provided, but not too close, because then we burned our legs in the process. I was constantly worried about having an accident and setting the house on fire, so I bought a metal screen to keep the fire safe. Unfortunately it also reduced the heat we received.

We found it difficult not to shake hands, not to say *bon appétit*, and not to ask questions that infringed on the privacy of others. If you met a stranger in Hungary you could expect that in the first five minutes he would ask what

In England

your salary was, how much you had paid for your house, for your car, and so on. Such questions were strictly taboo in England. We realised that many of our new friends wanted to know our 'story', and why and how we had left Hungary, but they didn't ask. To help the situation we usually volunteered the information and could see that our frankness was much appreciated.

Hungarian people like to complain. I would go as far as suggesting that it is one of their national characteristics. They complain about the economy, goods and services, officials, public transport, and more. If you ask a Hungarian how he is, he will reel off a long list of ailments. He is having pain in his left leg, he can't sleep at nights, his blood pressure is high, and he has to take medication for his cholesterol. Nobody feels sorry for him, but it provides a good basis to start a conversation. You ask an Englishmen the same question and the answer is without exception 'very well, thank you.' How can you start a conversation after that? In England, conversation between strangers as well as between friends always starts with the weather. 'It's cold today, isn't it?' 'Yesterday we had a nice day though.' 'We had more rain this April than the whole of last year, don't you think?' You had to give an answer, and there you were, talking to each other.

Every office worker was served tea in the office. My boss had some stomach problems and had to drink in between meals, Consequently he arranged to get two cups of tea instead of one. When I shared an office with him, he decided to order two cups for me as well, which meant that he now got a full pot. Unfortunately I couldn't manage to drink two cups and after a few weeks of trying I had to cancel the arrangement. He was not amused.

I was thrilled when a colleague of mine said 'You and your wife must come around to us sometime for tea.' Taking him literally, we were planning our visit for the next weekend before discovering that such an open-ended invitation is meaningless. However, one day he added a date, and so it became a real invitation..

When I told one of my English colleague that, as a foreigner, I was expected to be paid less than the natives, he explained that English workers would not tolerate such a thing. This was news to me. Later I learned the power of the trade unions.

Nobody in Hungary would ever make fun of their country. Jokes about the police, the Jews, Gypsies, and women are fair game, but not their country. Given any occasion, people would start marching with the national flag flying, and as soon as a crowd gathered in a square they would always sing the national anthem even if they weren't demonstrating about a national issue. Hungarians feel that they have to show their patriotism. And so we found it strange that in England people were happy making fun of their country, and would laugh at jokes for which you would be prosecuted in Hungary. But we soon realised that this was a strength rather than a weakness, and we started to value the honesty and sincerity of the people, their love for fairness and privacy, and their devotion to their customs and heritage.

We found that in England everything was the other way round to what we were used to. Traffic drove on the left. Forks were used upside down. Light switches, door locks, all worked the other way. People dressed formally during the week and casually on Sunday. Titles such as PhD were placed after the name. Vera and I used to say to each other 'If you don't know how to do something, do it the other way to how you think it should be done.' As a scientist I was already familiar with some of the English units, like Fahrenheit and pounds per square inch, but had not come

In England

across them in everyday use.

We bought a small black and white TV set (there were no colours yet) and learned a lot about English (and American) life from it. But when I said to a friend that I was learning English from the popular programme *The Life & Legend of Wyatt Earp* he started laughing. The TV also helped to keep István happy while he had to wait for us in the house. We used to watch *The Black & White Minstrel Show* and even enjoyed the advertisements. I still remember the jingles ('The Esso sign means happy motoring...' and 'You'll wonder where the yellow went when you brush your teeth with Pepsodent'), but I couldn't understand why a serious musician playing the violin or the trumpet also had to act the clown. In Hungary, serious music never mixed with other forms of entertainment, especially the lighter kind.

The fact that we lived in the north of England made settling down much easier. People were more friendly and seemed to have more time, patience, and even interest in others. Vera liked to be called 'love' by the bus conductor instead of 'madam' as was customary in the south. My brother-in-law and his family stayed in London but didn't feel as settled as we did. Later they emigrated to Canada, and in Toronto they found lots of other Hungarians. Their GP, dentist, hairdresser, travel agent and more are all Hungarians. They eat only Hungarian food, have only Hungarian friends, and I think they are missing a lot out of life.

Our friends came partly from work, partly from the neighbourhood. We wanted to start life afresh and joined the local congregational church, and we found the people there very helpful. There was a National Refugee Day organised, and the minister asked Vera to make a speech from the pulpit. She declined but recommended me, and indeed I did it. I remember the last sentence: I said it was a much happier feeling to give than to receive. Afterwards, they wanted to bypass me with the collection tray, but I insisted on contributing 10/-. Talking of the collection tray, it used to be passed from neighbour to neighbour in each pew. We used to sit at the back of the church, and by the time the tray reached us it was pretty full. I don't know how, but we managed one time to drop it between us, all the coins rolling about and making a terrible noise. We prayed that the floor would open and swallow us, but of course it didn't happen. We went down on all fours scrabbling to catch what we could, but were told not to worry, that it would still be there after the service.

To complete our plan for assimilation, we had István baptised at the age of eight. He went to Sunday school until he was twelve, when he decided not to go anymore. When he told Vera about his decision and saw the disappointment in her eyes, he put his arms around her and asked 'But you still love me, don't you?' Soon after that I too dropped out, but Vera continued going to church until we moved into a new area.

We had a few pounds saved up from our work in the camp, but it wasn't enough to live on until the end of the month when the salaries were paid. I had to ask for an advance, which was most unusual in England. To begin with they wanted me to pay it all back at the end of the month from my first salary, leaving me once more with almost nothing to live on. I managed to persuade them to give me another month in advance, and to deduct it in instalments from the next three months' salaries. This was enough to get us going.

Because of our financial situation, but also because of our background, Vera too was looking for a job. She went to interviews wearing clothes which she had received from the Women's Voluntary Service. This charity also gave us other

In England

things, such as a metal bedstead, toilet paper, and even a jar of Hungarian paprika. God only knows where they got it from. My landlady, Mrs Brown, used to help Vera with her appearance and also made up her hair. At one interview they asked her if I was a member of a golf club; at another they objected to her having a young son. Eventually she got a job with Kellogg's Cornflakes in Trafford Park. Their product was unknown in Hungary at that time. Every month, all employees received packets of their various products free of charge, and we gave them all away.

There was a lot of smog in those days, caused by burning coal, and Manchester had more than its fair share of this unpleasantness. The Kellogg's offices were separated from the factory by a public road, and occasionally Vera had to go over for some information.

'How can I cross the road in this fog?' she asked her boss one day.

'You just have to take a chance and run,' was his answer.

Kellogg's was an American company, and working practices were very different from those we had in Hungary. Vera was put to work in the department of commercial statistics, producing tables and graphs of production and sales volumes. Unfortunately her first boss was a real bastard. He used to check how long an employee spent in the bathroom and occasionally reprimanded Vera for staying longer than the allowed five minutes. Fortunately after a few months he was demoted and she got a new one who appreciated her talents and her accuracy when working with figures.

Vera too suffered from not having mastered English, but she had a nice colleague, a married woman, who helped her with choosing food in the canteen: 'Stay with your tray behind me in the queue, and every time I choose a dish just say "the same please".'

WHERE IS MY HOME?

She was one of those slim girls who could eat like a horse and still wouldn't get fat. Vera did as she suggested, and duly put on a lot of weight. One day the manager of the personnel department approached her with a letter from Sweden. It was obviously written in Swedish, but he asked Vera to translate it.

'But it's in Swedish,' she protested.

'I know,' said the manager, 'but you're a foreigner too.'

The next problem was to find someone to look after our son. There was a local nursery, and Vera took him there, but the matron was most reluctant to accept him because he spoke no English at all. Eventually she conceded, and after a couple of weeks he was correcting our pronunciation. He laughed at us, because we couldn't say 'matron' properly. The weekends were still a problem, as we had to work most Saturdays, when the nursery was closed. We turned to the family where I was lodging, and Bill Brown, a travelling salesman of agricultural equipment, used to take István with him. Unfortunately István was a very poor traveller and was often sick in Bill's car. Eventually we found an old lady, Mrs Applestone, who for a small charge was prepared to come to our house and look after our son from the time school ended to when one of us got home. She suggested that while she was baby-sitting she could do some ironing for us as well. Vera gave her our newly acquired electric iron, but this was no good: she would only use the old-fashioned type you had to fill with hot charcoal. Mrs Applestone was a very reliable lady, but one day Vera found an old gentleman in her place, sitting next to István, both watching television. Vera got quite worked up, but the gentleman turned out to be the boyfriend of Mrs Applestone, who was busy and couldn't come. Afterwards István asked us if in future the

In England

gentleman could come more often, as he didn't talk as much as Mrs Applestone.

During the summer holidays we sent István to a camp for children, located in Chichester, close by the south coast. It was rather expensive, but we had no other choice. Fortunately, he liked being there, found the organised excursions interesting, and, after returning home, he would talk endlessly about Tintagel Castle, King Arthur, and the Round Table. Unfortunately, not all the children at the camp came from a stable home, but he didn't pick up any bad habits from the others.

Vera's role was harder than mine: working full-time with occasional overtime as well, looking after the house, cooking, washing, etc., and, on top of all this, continuously worrying about István, who had to find his way home from school and who occasionally waited alone in the house for one of us to return. Once he called Vera, who was still in the office, to say that he had been stung by a wasp. She could only advise him to walk down to the shops where there was a chemist and ask for some ointment. He had to learn independence at an early age.

Did we miss anything of Hungary? One might immediately think of the weather. England was famous for its rainy weather, quite different from what we were used to in Hungary, where rain lasted a few hours, maybe half a day, but then was over. In Manchester the amount of rain was not necessarily *more*, but it took a lot longer for it to come down. Drizzle, as it is called, was unknown to us. However, a coin has two sides and we found the mild winters and pleasantly warm summers in England better than the extremes in Hungary.

Until we got our car, we missed the cheap public transport in Budapest, which covered the whole city and its surroundings. In spite of the continued availability of fruit and vegetables, we found they tasted less authentic than the Hungarian varieties, albeit that these were only available when in season. We especially missed paprika, both fresh as a vegetable and as a sun-dried, ground seasoning. They are very healthy: Professor Szentgyörgyi even received a Nobel prize for extracting vitamin C from the Hungarian paprika. Later on, when visitors from Hungary were allowed, we always asked them to bring fresh paprika for us.

We did at least find an Austrian shop in London, where we could buy things unavailable in Manchester, such as a poppy-seed grinder. This *mákdaráló* is a very important tool in making *bejgli*, the traditional Hungarian Christmas cake, and we still use ours even today. We could also buy other kitchen utensils to slice marrows and to make a traditional pasta dish called *nokedli*, and all sorts of spices, including paprika powder. Life became just a little more pleasant.

Before our English improved we missed going to the cinema and the theatre, so we focused our attention on concerts and bought season tickets to the Halle Orchestra, which played in the Free Trade Hall with Sir John Barbirolli conducting. He was an excellent conductor, but by then already an old man and towards the end of each performance he presumably got tired and would occasionally hit the stand in front of him with his baton. Later, when our English got better, we also visited the Library Theatre.

We missed our kayak, but not our walks in the Budapest hills: in England we used to walk instead out at Alderly Edge and did some more serious hiking in the hills of Derbyshire after work, when in summer the days were longer. All colleagues and wives were welcome, and Vera joined me and the rest whenever she could. Of course, the walk always ended in a pub.

In England

To start with I missed the few Hungarian books which I had used during my university studies. There was a bookshop in London selling left-wing literature, which obviously had close contacts with communist countries including Hungary. Through them I could get hold of my books once more. My mother-in-law had to give them for free to a bookshop in Hungary, and I had to buy them back again in hard currency when they arrived in London. By the time they arrived, I didn't need them so much. Until our English improved we read Hungarian books, but after our son started school we gradually switched to English, though we still speak Hungarian between ourselves at home.

Did we miss our family and friends? I didn't miss my relatives, because I had never really had any lasting contact, never mind a relationship, with any one of them. Vera of course missed her brother, but no other relatives. We missed our old friends, of whom more later. She also missed Budapest, where she was born and had spent a happy childhood. Looking back on it, settling down in England and integrating into local life was not without pain, but it was worth it. We never once thought that we had made a mistake by leaving Hungary and coming to England. We found that Parkinson's adage that 'expenditure expands to meet income' turned out to be true, and we took our increased standard of living as our new normality. Still, we were all the time aware of the fact that we were aliens in a foreign country.

2

The First Eight Years

A FEW DAYS after I started work for Shell, there was a serious accident involving an explosion and fire at the plant. It was the weekend, and I phoned my boss at home saying I was ready to help, if it was needed. This would have been the normal thing to do in Hungary, but my boss said that the problem was under control and I would only be in the way. Obviously Shell was prepared for such emergencies and had trained people to deal with them.

I was working in the scheduling section of the economics and scheduling department. My line manager was Ken, a good administrator, very efficient and accurate, but without any technical education. During his long service, he picked up all that was necessary. He was a tall, slim man, approaching fifty, who suffered from a chronic stomach problem. This made him rather serious and sour and, what was worse, more than a bit malodorous from his various gases. The department head, Mr Venis, was a short, middle-aged man with a quick wit, but he was a real bastard with his own staff as well as with his colleagues. Nobody liked him, and this made his cooperation with other department heads a little shaky. Unfortunately, to begin with this affected my own relationship with other departments as well.

We had to get the most essential utensils and furniture for our rented house, which was very poorly furnished. My boss Ken sold me some crockery, some of it chipped and cracked, but it served us well for years. I also agreed to buy a second-hand wardrobe from Mr Venis. I made arrangements with a transport company and took the day off from work to receive it. In the morning I got a phone call.

'When are you going to pay me?' asked Mr Venis.

'When I receive the wardrobe, of course,' I answered.

'That's not good enough. You have to pay before it leaves my house.'

I was flabbergasted, and very suspicious that there was something wrong with the furniture.

'And what can I do if it arrives damaged? If we have a disagreement, who can I complain to?' I asked

'Nobody will believe you, you bloody foreigner!'

This summed up my department head. I realised I had no choice. I went to his house, paid him, and in the end the furniture turned out to be OK.

Mr Venis collected cacti for a hobby, and one year for his birthday the staff presented him with an unusual specimen. Mr Venis was very pleased with his present and showed it to everyone, quoting its Latin name. Unfortunately after a few days it started to die. It turned out that the staff had played a trick on him by cutting off the top of a pineapple and planting it in soil so it looked like a cactus!

Our job was to provide the manufacturing plant with the monthly, five-quarterly, and yearly operating budgets, which were originally designed by my boss and kept in the same form year after year. It worked reasonably well in the beginning, when the location consisted of a few factory units only, but with rapid expansion however the complexity had increased and the tables indicating the volume of materials no longer provided a clear picture. I had to show the weight of each component of a gas as it moved around the factory, making sure that at the end it all added up. I hated the work because it was tedious and repetitive and, what's more, irrelevant. I regularly made small mistakes which were discovered by my boss, and once I was warned that I could lose my job because of them. So when Ken went on holiday I decided to simplify the tables. I was able to draw from my experience in the design office in Hungary, where I had

The First Eight Years

worked with similar tables. On his return, Ken was furious at first but later admitted that I was right and from then on kept to the new method.

Apart from the official lunch and tea breaks, work was continuous and quite different from the working practices I had got used to in Hungary, where I could visit the buffet any time during the day. In the canteen we had a cooked meal every day, followed by a sweet such as bread and butter pudding or an ice-cream. I especially loved the chocolate-covered ice-cream, and one hot afternoon during tea break I walked over to the canteen, which I found strangely closed. Luckily there was someone around and I managed to buy a bar of my favourite choc-ice. Unfortunately on my return I had to go and see my bosses on a technical matter. They didn't say anything, but I'm sure they were surprised to see me munching on the ice-cream.

Shell maintained a policy of job rotation, and Mr Venis had a reputation for giving a bad report on the people he wanted to keep, so no other department would want them. Later I learned that he did this to me as well. Fortunately from time to time all graduates were invited for a discussion with the Works Manager, Mr Huggit, and when my time came I think I made a good impression on him. He offered me the compulsory cup of tea and asked about my background, my technical training and experience. He also inquired about my decision to leave Hungary and why I had come to England. I told him that I had relatives in America but wanted to remain in Europe, in spite of the much higher salaries over there. 'Money isn't everything,' I concluded, and he agreed with me.

He asked me about how I got on with Mr Venis, saying that he knew him to be a difficult character, but a good expert. I didn't complain. He asked me which department I might want to go next. After I explained what

WHERE IS MY HOME?

I did in Hungary he transferred me to the Technological Department. This was the elite of the whole plant. It was led by a chief technologist, Alex, and his deputy, Brian, a brilliant scientist. Brian had been injured in the accident just after I had started work and had burns on his face. Alex was continuously busy as part of the management team and had no time or wish to get involved with day-to-day operations. I only met him at official Christmas parties. Then there were two section heads, Peter and Len, leading a number of young graduates. Since in England graduate chemists and engineers could finish their university education at the age of 22, I was the oldest amongst them. They were all bright and motivated and there was a real sense of teamwork. I shared an office with John P., a young, lively, and intelligent scientist, just married to a nurse. We got on very well and had occasionally visited each other socially with our wives. He also helped me to learn to drive by sitting in my car

From right: Morris, Hazel, Peter, Cathy

as a passenger. Another member of our team was Charles, who came from a family of army officers. He had attended Wellington College, a military school, and was a member of the TA. He was short, serious, and single.

There was also a Scottish couple among us—Ian Christy, a technologist, and his wife Adah, who worked in the laboratory. We developed a friendship and often visited each other. They both helped us to learn to drive. Later they left Shell, Ian obtained a teacher's diploma, and returned to Scotland to teach science at St Andrews' Grammar School. I couldn't understand his decision, since he was a good technologist, liked by everyone.

'Why are you leaving such a good job?' I asked.

'Because I love fishing. A very cheap but time-consuming hobby,' he replied.

They settled down in no time, never regretting the move. Later he accepted an assignment to teach in Malta and spent a year there with his family. Because they couldn't take their Yorkshire terrier Gay with them we volunteered to look after her. It was fortunate that by the time we had to move to Holland they had returned, but more about that later. We still keep in contact.

My direct boss, Peter Croft, was a very nice person; we had regular social contact with him and with his wife and invited each other round for dinner. Cathy, his wife, was a good cook and I especially liked her steak-and-kidney pie, a dish unknown in Hungary. In return they very much enjoyed Vera's *borjú pörkölt*, a veal goulash. In Hungary dinner parties had been unknown, because most people had very limited accommodation, and so people had entertained friends in cafés and restaurants. Because labour was cheap, the price of a restaurant meal had not been much more than the sum of its ingredients. Vera now had to learn to cook and she managed to do it in a very short time. Her mother couldn't cook, and in Hungary we had never entertained, nor had we eaten in expensive restaurants.

We developed a friendly relationship with another couple too, and the six of us used to visit each other in turn. Morris was a very clever and very ambitious young scientist who later switched to finance and was eventually promoted to the prestigious "A" grade. His wife Hazel was an attractive woman who looked after her appearance and knew how to behave coquettishly. Peter rather fancied her, and one evening in our living room, seated next to each other on the sofa, he jokingly asked her if he could kiss her. Hazel was game, and the two of them engaged in a long, passionate kiss, after which they both acted as if nothing had happened. It was all for show only, and his wife Cathy said nothing. Still, I wouldn't have wanted to be in his shoes after they went home.

Peter and I had regular arguments at work over technical matters, but also on planning and organising. His background was in manufacturing, which made him careful and conservative. I was prepared to take more risks in trying out new ideas. On one occasion, a day when they were due to come to us for dinner, we had an almighty row and I told Vera not to expect them, but they turned up cheerfully, not mentioning our disagreement once. He was one of four people who recommended us for naturalisation and also asked us to be godparents to their youngest son, not knowing that we were secular Jews!

One time, Peter organised a trip for all the men in his section to visit a nightclub, where the main attraction was a 'Miss Ding Dong Bell'. As the name suggests, she had enormous breasts, which she slowly uncovered to great applause. They served drinks during the show, and instead of a glass they provided a whole bottle. At the end of the show the waitresses charged for the amount missing from the bottle, which they checked by shining a torch across it and making a guess.

Three of my colleagues invited me to join them on a pub crawl, a tour I was unfamiliar with. John drove us from pub to pub, and at each place each of us drank half a pint of bitter. There were eight pubs in the area, and after each visit the three of them debated the beer they served. Sometime they had disagreements and wanted to go back for a second opinion, but apparently this was against the rules. To me all English beer tasted the same, so I didn't participate in the discussion. English people don't eat anything during serious drinking, but I would have liked to eat something, perhaps some potato chips, and I soon started to feel the effect of the alcohol, but not John, who insisted that the beer didn't affect his driving. 'I know I've had a drink, so I drive slower and more carefully,' he explained.

At the time the law didn't set a legal limit and there were no breathalysers, but today he would be prosecuted for less. I braved the drinking, but had to throw up as soon as I got home.

Our job was to solve all sorts of problems in the manufacturing plant, and there were frequent meetings involving the whole group. This was a pleasant and welcome change from my experience in Hungary. On one of these occasions I made a comment on a plan, starting something like: 'I believe we should….' The assistant chief technologist came down on me like a ton of bricks: 'I'm not interested in your belief; this isn't a church!' Looking back on it, he was wrong. People, especially in research, should listen to their intuition.

On the whole we did a good job, solved many problems, and improved the efficiency of the plant, but we also made mistakes. The biggest blunder of my whole career was when

WHERE IS MY HOME?

I wanted to try out a new process, based on extensive tests in the laboratory, followed by several runs at the pilot plant to make sure that it worked, before applying it on the large manufacturing reactor. Unfortunately it didn't work, and a solid block of hard plastic got wrapped around the stirrer, forming a huge lollipop. It took a week to dig it all out using pneumatic drills. In Hungary I would have been sent to prison for this, accused of being an agent for the CIA, and I thought that even in England I would at least have been sacked on the spot. To my surprise I wasn't even blamed. It was just one of those things that happened when the scale-up of pilot-plant data went wrong. It took some time, but finally we understood the reason for the failure and got a lot of useful knowledge from it.

I never felt inferior to my English colleagues; as far as I could judge, their scientific knowledge was about the same as mine, but they were far ahead of me where economics were involved. I found, however, a big difference in the abilities of the shift foremen. In Hungary the factories were run by graduates, in England by shift foremen, who were expected to use much more initiative. The gap between the roles and abilities of the graduates and non-graduates was much greater in Hungary, where it was not uncommon to use graduates as shift foremen. This gap was partly due to education, which in Hungary concentrated on universities, but partly to the attitude of management, which was authoritarian. I found the power of the trade unions very different to what it was in Hungary. The fact that there were several unions was also strange, and it took a long time to understand the thinking behind 'restrictive practices'. An operator, for example, was allowed to use a spanner to open and close his reactor, but he was not allowed to change a burned-out lamp: for that he had to call in the electricians. I couldn't find any evidence for what I had heard in Hungary about the sufferings of the proletariat under capitalism. If anything, the workers performed at a more leisurely pace than they did in Hungary. What was strikingly different was the quality of the equipment and materials used.

Once, I had almost finished an important experiment when a pipe transporting light plastic balls got blocked at a bend. In such occasions the correct procedure was to call for the pipe fitters, who would inspect it and call the riggers to build a supporting structure. Then they would open the pipe, allow the operator to blow out the blockage with compressed air and put it back in its place. Unfortunately the whole process could have lasted several hours and in the meantime operations would have to stop and we would have to start the experiment from scratch. I decided not to follow procedure but to carry out the work myself. After about five minutes work I was able to continue and soon finished the experiment. Unfortunately someone reported this to the trade-union convener, who almost called a strike because I had ignored the rule regarding restrictive practices. Only by claiming that I was an ignorant foreigner, who didn't know better, did I manage to save the peace.

The Technological Department organised a formal dinner-dance every year for all staff members and their partners. Members of the management were also invited. Neither Vera nor I were good dancers. We could manage a slow tango and the waltz, but not the faster quickstep, so we joined forces with the Nichols to practise at their home. It was a sad affair, since they were even worse than us and we were continuously treading on each other's feet. At the party we had to wear smoking jackets with bow-ties, while the ladies came in cocktail dresses, and we all drove to a nice restaurant outside Manchester. After dinner there was dancing and the party always ended with a conga. I had no smoking jacket and bought one from a cheap warehouse in

WHERE IS MY HOME?

Oldham Street. Vera too bought a cocktail dress of green chiffon, with a design of flowers. She looked very nice in it, but to her horror another woman had exactly the same dress. I don't really understand why this was considered a near disaster: all the men were wearing exactly the same outfit and none of us complained.

In Hungary I had made and sold perfumes and face-creams to earn enough money to get better accommodation. Consequently, my old colleagues were convinced that in England I would become a very successful businessman, but they were wrong. I couldn't have made a living from making cosmetics like I had in Hungary, and I couldn't compete with the big, established companies. Doing illegal business as in Hungary was out of the question. But, most importantly, in England I could live well on my salary, I could get good accommodation; I didn't want more, and I had no desire to become a millionaire.

Having completed one year at Shell I was eligible for a 100% mortgage with a company guarantee, and we bought our first house in Sale, five miles southwest of Manchester city centre, for £1,800. It took a long time to have all the paperwork and approvals completed, and the seller grew suspicious that I might not be a serious buyer. One day he came to see me and was only satisfied when I showed him a letter from Shell with my salary on. Our new house in Sale was a modest, semi-detached house with a small garden, in a quiet street, but it had everything we needed, including three bedrooms. I could swear that the birds sang even more beautifully there than at our rented house. One day before we had to move, one of our soon-to-be ex-neighbours invited us for coffee the next evening. English people need a lot of time to make a commitment by inviting strangers to their home.

The First Eight Years

Our first house in Sale

The famous English saying that 'my house is my castle' could also be rephrased as 'my house is my work camp.' This was the first time that we as a married couple had had a house of our own, and we soon realised the 'pleasures' of gardening, cutting the lawn, painting and decorating, and so forth. In Hungary, with the very few exceptions of large estates, nobody had a lawn, only a small bed of flowers at the front of the house. Lawns were considered a waste of resources, and all available space was turned over to fruit and vegetables. Our new next-door neighbour was Uncle Joe, who taught me how to do all these things. He used to hold the ladder while I painted the outside of the house. To him, the only colours to use were green and white, so that's what I used.

After we bought our house, it was time for us too to learn to drive. In those days we had to give hand signals if we wanted to change direction or slow down. We both

WHERE IS MY HOME?

Our first car

took some lessons from a local driving instructor whenever he was sober enough. In addition we were helped to learn by colleagues. I passed my test first time and we bought a second-hand Ford Popular for £300. It had only the very basics required by law, for example a single windscreen wiper for the driver's side, but we were satisfied. A few weeks later Vera called me at work: 'If you get home first, you might not find our car on the driveway. Don't call the police, it isn't stolen, it's with me.' This was how she broke the news that she too had passed her test first time.

The car made a big difference to our lives. We explored the country, first going to the seaside in North Wales, later south to Devon and Cornwall. On a warm, summer's day sitting on the beach I even got mild sunstroke, the only time in my life. We went north to the Lake District and thought that it was the most beautiful scenery in the world until we went to Scotland. Occasionally the engine overheated and we had to call the AA for help, but we managed to get up to Ross and Cromarty and back again. We also took Joyce our English teacher and her old mother to Chester Zoo, which they enjoyed very much. Once, travelling in Scotland, we saw a sign on a police station, opposite Burns' house in Edinburgh. It read:

POLICE
Department of
ALIENS, FIREARMS And
DANGEROUS DRUGS

England and the English were very tolerant, but we had to accept the fact that everybody was suspicious about the unknown, and this included foreigners like us.

At about this time both my mother and mother-in-law got permission from the Hungarian government to leave the country. They were old and a burden on the country's pension fund and health service. Because my mother had nowhere else to go, she came to live with us, while my mother-in-law went to live with her son and family in London. They were allowed to bring with them only their personal belongings, and even that up to a ridiculously low limit only. An official was present during their packing and valued each item. My mother bribed the man and managed to bring out a little more, but my mother-in-law was not as enterprising.

Neither of these grandmothers were happy in their new environment, and a lot of friction resulted. Eventually my mother left to look after the household of a widowed man with two young children, and our relationship immediately improved. After my brother-in-law emigrated to Canada, my mother-in-law remained alone in a small flat in London. Eventually both grandmothers died in England. I heard a joke, about a grandmother who was spending six months with one child in America and six months with her other child in Europe; twice a year she travelled from one to the other. When asked where she felt most happy, she answered: 'on the way....'

For our first holiday we consulted a booklet full of advertisements and chose a private address in Cornwall. It was a small guest house with a few families as guests and had one small dining room. However, our landlady, a young, jovial but badly dressed woman, served our meals in the living room and I was wondering why not with the rest of the guests? Then I looked at the books on the shelves and realised why: most were communist literature, written by Marx, Lenin, and the like. The whole guesthouse was a holiday resort for members of the British Communist Party, and we were the only guests not belonging to the Party. They had advertised their guesthouse only once in an old booklet, and by an ironic chance we had picked that particular one! As it turned out, they respected us and didn't force any political arguments upon us. Because there were several children, István liked the place very much and we all had a good holiday.

Our next holiday was in South Wales, and we selected a guesthouse with the attractive name Picton Park from another, more up-to-date guidebook. We were expecting the house to stand in the middle of the park, but alas, a name was only a name. The house hadn't even got a front garden: it was right on a busy street. It was a large house and there were six couples as guests, and once the children were in bed all the adults went to the local pub for a drink. Or, to be precise, we didn't go for *a* drink, we went *to* drink.

English pubs had to close at 10.30pm in those days, and ten minutes before that a bell was rung with the famous announcement from the barman: 'Last orders, gentlemen, please!' But this was a small village, and the owner of the pub signalled us to go to another room with the sign on the door that read 'Private'. When all the other guests had gone, we could sneak back in and continue drinking. Local custom demanded that each man in turn bought a 'round' of drinks, a practice unfamiliar to me. I couldn't keep pace with the rate of drinking, and full pints of bitter accumulated in front of me. Still, when my turn came, I too had to order a round. To aid serious drinking, the owner brought in some food as well. It was 'faggots' the Welsh answer to the Scottish Haggis.

Before we qualified for UK passports we each had a document, a sort of convention, stating that we were refugees, but that we were living in the United Kingdom, and that the United Kingdom was prepared to take us back if we were to travel abroad. Before visiting any country, we had to have a visa first, which was no problem, but it had to be obtained in the United Kingdom in advance of the travel. For our first foreign holiday, we decided to go to Spain's Costa Brava. The husband of our secretary at Shell ran a travel business, and he made all the bookings for us. I asked for a Spanish visa and a French transit visa with double entry, because the plane was landing in Perpignan. He got the Spanish visa for us, but said that we didn't need a French visa because right after landing we would be boarding a Spanish bus for the Costa Brava. We arrived in Perpignan at about midnight and the French asked for our visas. We wanted to buy one there, but it was not possible. 'Could we spend the night in jail?' asked Vera in desperation, 'and tomorrow buy a visa in town?' But it was no good. They put us on the same plane and promptly returned us to Manchester. Next morning I went early to work and waited at the entrance for our travel agent, who brought his wife to work in his car. He got the shock of his life seeing me, but accepted responsibility and we returned a week later to Spain at no extra cost. In the meantime I went to the French consulate in Liverpool, paid the 10/- fee, and got the visas without a single question asked. They were even very sympathetic to our plight, when I told them what happened.

We stayed in Estartit on the Costa Brava, in a so-called 'hotel', which was a converted house belonging to the local lawyer. The trouble was, a renovation was still in progress and the owner had no idea how to run a hotel for English holidaymakers. We booked a single room for our son, but this turned out to be the old toilet, with a tiny window almost at ceiling level. The food was atrocious. Once, we had *paella* made from chicken instead of fish. One of the guests found the head of the chicken on his plate and banged the skull-bone with his spoon, complaining. Eventually some of the guests were moved to a proper hotel, but we decided to stay for the remaining three days of our holiday.

At his request I took István to a bullfight, but to his credit he was disgusted and we left before the end. Much later I attended a lecture about bullfights and was assured that the bull was being revered as a symbol of strength and

On holiday in Spain

The First Eight Years

heroism. In response to the question of why the bull always had to die at the end, the lecturer answered: 'And what about an opera? Everybody knows at the start that Gilda, the daughter of Rigoletto, will die, but still people come and see it again and again.' This was true, but in the opera Gilda isn't pierced with darts before she's killed, and we don't see any blood mopped up with sawdust.

When I registered for military service in Hungary, I received a small booklet with all my personal details, which, amongst other things, stated that I was not a member of the Communist Party. This was because I had been expelled during the purge of 1948 or 1949 and the document was issued in 1952. It was to become a very valuable document, because it provided the only proof that I was not a member of the Communist Party. When, in England in 1957, I was interviewed by the British immigration office, I produced all my documents, including this one. There was a Hungarian interpreter, who saw that I was not a Party member in 1952, nevertheless, he asked the standard question:

'When did you join the Party?' It was obviously a trick question, because he had absolutely no knowledge of the facts. He probably expected that I might give a date after 1952. In Hungary I would have replied without hesitation that I had never been a member. But this was England, and I decided to tell the truth and never regretted it. The only time my ex-membership of the Party caused inconvenience was when we visited the USA. We had to fill in a form in advance, and one of the questions was: 'Are you or have you ever been a member of an organisation… like the Communist Party?' I answered honestly with a 'yes', which meant that I had to go to the US consulate in Amsterdam to apply for a visa. I was interrogated by an official who wanted to know why I had joined the Party.

WHERE IS MY HOME?

'Because I was an anti-fascist,' I said, but this didn't seem to the official to be an adequate reason.

'Did you join because otherwise you couldn't get a job?' he asked further.

'I was 17 years old and a student at the grammar school,' I said, but he didn't give up.

'Perhaps otherwise you wouldn't get enough food?'

'Anyone who's used this argument to justify his membership was lying to you,' I answered, almost angrily now. It was obvious that he wanted to help me by finding an acceptable 'excuse', but eventually he had enough and gave us a special visa. Arriving on a Greyhound bus at the US frontier from Canada, we were the only passengers who were ordered off the bus and into the office building. After more interrogation we were allowed back. We returned several times to America, each time with a one-off visa, and visited almost all its beautiful national parks. Today we don't need to have a visa: Middle Eastern terrorists now pose a greater danger than ex-communists.

The second time I was interviewed about my Hungarian past concerned my knowledge of Hungarian industry, and I told them what I knew. For a moment I thought they also wanted to get some valuable technical information from me, but later I realised that all I knew was old hat. Fortunately we were now approaching the end of our initial five-year residence period and were allowed to apply for naturalisation. We had a third interview, conducted by a friendly detective. We told him everything truthfully. We needed four sponsors, all born in England, but by then these were not difficult for us to find. One of them was the husband of my old landlady, and when they next visited us she said jokingly: 'A policeman came and enquired about you, George. I asked him "what has he done this time?"' Our other sponsors were Roy, our first neighbour, and two colleagues, Peter Croft and Geoff Nichols.

I was glad I had nothing to hide, and after about nine months' waiting we took the oath and received our precious documents, and were allowed to apply for a British passport. So ended our roles as stateless refugees, and we started our new life as British citizens. As far as I could see, we integrated well into British society, were very happy, felt accepted by the locals, and made many friends. István was well on the way to being assimilated, and to feeling more English than Hungarian. I never thought of ever leaving England for another country.

After nursery school, István attended school in Sale. So far I have been calling my son István, because this is his given name, but when we settled in England he wanted to be called Stephen. At an early age he realised the disadvantages of being a foreigner. Young boys can be very cruel, and he didn't want to be different from the majority. I tried to keep his knowledge of Hungarian alive, but he wanted to talk only English. When he could read, I bought him a book read by every Hungarian boy, but he was not interested. I offered to read it for him, but at every second word he stopped me to ask its meaning. I'd thought that knowing another language would come in useful for an Englishman, but eventually I had to give up.

It was at this time that dark clouds started to gather on the horizon of our carefree lives. Vera wanted another child. Back in Hungary, neither of us had thought that a second child was a good idea, and after we had arrived in England penniless we first had to build up our new life. Now we had reached that stable situation when a second child would indeed be a reasonable thing to want. But by this time István was seven years old, and I was very much aware that I hadn't had a relationship with my own brother, also seven years older than myself, until I had reached the age of fifteen and he twenty-two. I concluded that we had left it too late, and that the two children would never grow up together. I was also worried that, after the second, Vera would want a third, and that the situation would simply repeat itself.

Vera though didn't accept my argument and took every opportunity to persuade me. She talked to our GP and enlisted the help of my department head, but I didn't give in. Who was right? To this date Vera regrets my decision and brings it up every time she feels low, and it gives me a guilty feeling. We are very much alone now, having no relatives in Holland. I suppose loneliness is a price we have had to pay for leaving our homeland. I would say, though, that it's the only price. We could have been lucky with a second healthy and loving child, but we could also have created a lot of potential problems. The odds were against us because of our blood groups: I am o/Rhesus positive, and Vera is o/Rhesus negative. I understand now what we didn't know then—that in such a case a second child born to the same mother can develop a potentially fatal condition caused by having parents with these different blood types.

Another Hungarian woman refugee, Piri, joined the company where Vera worked. She was a good-looking young woman with the figure of a boy, having practically no bust. 'Most men are less interested in a woman's breasts than in her buttocks,' she used to say to Vera and, of course, her backside did have a perfect shape! She was hyperactive, always busy with something, impulsive with a rough edge. Occasionally she could hurt people with her quick and witty remarks, but she always apologised afterwards. She had married young, and in 1956 had escaped not only from the communists but also from her husband, and had fled

The First Eight Years

with her lover, Bandi. Later she divorced her husband and married Bandi, who was her exact opposite: quiet and slow, debating and weighing up everything before making any decision. He dressed as a true businessman, which went well with his impeccable manners. Bandi might have been an excellent lover, but he turned out to be a lousy husband. Piri missed the excitement, and soon started an affair with Jack, one of the department heads at her work. I have no doubt in my mind who was the instigator. Piri kept a picture of Jack in her purse, and told Bandi that it was a picture of a distant but dear old relative of hers, living in Australia. He was, she said, a lousy letter writer, that's why they never received any news of him. But at the firm's next Christmas party Bandi recognised 'Uncle' Jack from Australia, dancing with his wife. One evening soon after the party he arrived at our door looking unusually excited.

'George, can I borrow your car?'

'Where do you want to go?' I asked, because I was just about to go out to collect Vera myself.

'I urgently need to get home, and our car is with my wife.' He stressed the word 'urgently'. 'I'll bring it back to you at once.'

'You know what?' I said. 'I'm going that way. I can give you a lift.'

We got into my car, and he told me the reason for this emergency. He had discovered the relationship between his wife and Jack and knew that the two of them were right then secretly meeting at a hotel. Bandi wanted to be home before Piri arrived. He asked me to stay just a while, to be of further service, if needed. When we arrived, he ran into his house and I parked my car around the corner. Soon after that, Piri arrived, and wanted to get into their house but couldn't. The bedroom window opened, and Bandi appeared for a moment. What happened next I shall never forget. First, a large suitcase came flying down from the still-open window, followed by several items of women's clothing, starting with the underwear. Then came the dresses, and finally an overcoat. Bandi obviously gave a lot of thought to what, and in which order, he should dispose of. Everything was landing on the street just in front of the house, and by this time all the neighbours were watching in amazement. At first Piri shouted at Bandi, but then she gave up and started packing her things into the suitcase.

That's when I had to make an appearance. I was supposed to give Piri a lift, but she wouldn't accept it. She had their car and the keys, and was not volunteering to leave them behind for Bandi. But she did at least accept my offer to stay with us until she could find some accommodation for herself. Jack, of course, accepted all responsibility for the mishap and offered to leave his own family, marry Piri, and keep her happy for the rest of her life. But the offer of marriage from an ardent lover sounded all too familiar to Piri, who declined it.

To have Piri staying was no problem to us. She went to work with Vera, gave her lifts, helped in the kitchen, and ate with us. One Sunday morning I went into the bathroom and found Piri lying naked in the bathtub.

'Sorry!' I said. 'The door was open!' And I turned immediately to go out, but she stopped me.

'Don't go, George, I want to ask you a favour.'

'What on earth could it be?' I remember thinking. Surely she didn't want to seduce me in my own home, in the presence of my wife?

'Would you please take a photo of me?' she said finally, without any shame. 'I want to save it for my old age, to remind me of how I looked when I was young.'

Later Bandi and Piri made up, and they lived in various countries where Bandi found work as a chemist, eventually

The First Eight Years

retiring to Spain. Bandi became mentally unstable, and once in a rage he broke up their car with a huge hammer. Soon after that he died. We phoned Piri: 'Why don't you move back to England? Why stay in a strange country all by yourself?'

'I stay because the cigarettes and the booze are cheaper here.' After this answer we lost contact.

Bandi had a crippled brother who had stayed in Hungary confined to a wheelchair and who collected stamps as a serious hobby. I had also been interested in stamps from my early childhood and started a correspondence and exchange with him. He would send me Hungarian stamps, which I had collected only up to 1945 because later issues had purely been money-spinners aimed at milking philatelists. In return I sent him colourful stamps mainly from the old British colonies. But he lived in communist Hungary, where the state kept an eye on any potential smuggling of valuables out of the country. Every exchange of stamps had to go via an official address, and the state controlled the value of stamps leaving and arriving in the country, the value coming in equalling or exceeding that leaving. Why was it that the same communists never applied the same principle to state-run businesses?

London seemed full of foreigners, and most Hungarians too had chosen to live there, but in Manchester it was quite unusual to hear someone talking Hungarian. When by chance I met Árpád and Juliska in one of the city's large stores on a Saturday I invited them to our house for supper. No, they said, they couldn't come. They had no Hungarian babysitter and the children didn't speak English. They had no car either, and public transport was unreliable late at night. So they came with their children for afternoon tea on Sunday and we visited them two weeks later.

WHERE IS MY HOME?

First, we had to admire their house from the outside, then Juliska's garden, and then we were led into their living-room. It was furnished with taste and modesty, using Hungarian hand-made knitwear as the only decoration. The door between the living-room and the dining-room was open and we could hear the familiar tunes of Hungarian gypsy music coming from a stereo tape-recorder. There were two such tape-recorders, both on the dining-room table in the middle of the room, together with a fabulous big wireless. There was no other furniture in the room at all.

'We haven't got enough money to buy a dining-room suite yet,' said Árpád, noticing my surprise. 'I spent all our money on the best tape-recorders we could buy.'

'But why two?'

'Because I need two machines for editing the tapes. I record music off the radio, and the reception from Budapest isn't very good here, so I have to do a lot of editing. I borrow tapes from anyone I can and copy them, too. Have you got some by any chance?'

'But why two of these expensive gadgets? Would a cheaper model not do?' I asked, ignoring his request; I didn't have any tapes of Gypsy music.

'No! The recording is only as good as the poorest piece of equipment. So I can't afford to have a weak link in my system, you see.'

Those tape-recorders were their most treasured possessions; the machines kept them alive and sane. We saw no point in arguing with them, as they would never have understood that their behaviour was, in fact, part of a vicious circle. They had refused to integrate and to live a normal life, as a result of which they felt unsettled, and because they felt unsettled they were forced to seek what pleasure they could in this isolation. After leaving, Vera and I discussed the experience and agreed that unless they

The First Eight Years

broke out of that vicious circle they would never be able to accept life for what it was and would never be happy.

We were just the opposite. We adapted ourselves to our new surroundings with great success. We too found some of the English customs strange, of course, but we soon realised that we could never change the way of life of fifty million British people just to suit our own. Strange or not, we had to accept it as it was. And we found great pleasure in the compensations of living in a Western democracy. The politeness, tolerance, and sense of justice of the British were the things we valued most. It took us time, perhaps more than a year, even to understand what democracy was. And we very much treasured our newly acquired British passports and the chance for foreign travel. As I expected, though, Árpád didn't want to go through with the naturalisation process.

'What good is a British passport for, if you don't travel further than Blackpool, anyway? And the continuous fog, which covers the whole country, is so unhealthy.' No, they didn't want their children to go through an English education either. Learning to use silly units such as ounces and feet and furlongs? They would have had to start school the following September, so it was time to make a decision. They would move back to Hungary. Organising this took up the whole summer. They knew that life in Hungary would mean a lower standard of living, so Juliska learnt to operate a knitting machine, of which they bought two. They sold their house and most of their belongings and flew to Vienna, where they bought a Volkswagen mini-van. With the children's electric train-set on the roof, and the two tape-recorders under the seat, they finally went on their way.

Next Christmas we got a card from Árpád and Juliska. They were living with Juliska's mother in a two-room flat in

WHERE IS MY HOME?

Kőbánya, a not-too-desirable district of Budapest. Their car had been badly damaged in an accident and now they were waiting for spare parts to come from Germany. One of the two knitting machines had been confiscated at the frontier, together with a lot of knitting wool, as it was considered to be a commercial quantity and above the permitted quota for private use. But they were at home and happy. Everybody spoke Hungarian, ate Hungarian, drank Hungarian, and most importantly, sang Hungarian. They still have their two tape-recorders, and they have just managed to tape the Beatles' latest song. According to their children, everybody is crazy about them in Budapest.

Thanks to Shell's policy of job rotation it was time for me to move on again. After a very pleasant spell of working in the Technological Department I was to be sent to London for two years, working in the Process Development Department led by Mr Holliday. As was usual on such an occasion, we were invited to inspect the house we would be renting free-of-charge from Shell in Chessington, near London. It was a very nice house with a garden, and I made a list of the items I would need to make it complete. This was no problem, as Shell promised to give a generous settling-in allowance. We were advised to sell our house, again with all costs covered by Shell, and so we duly did. The only real problem was that Vera liked her job at Kellogg's but had to resign. She recommended another girl in her place. We bought everything we needed for our new home and said goodbye to friends and neighbours. On the day of my leaving party in a pub, I got a telephone call from my new boss: 'Don't come, because within three months the whole department will be transferring to Carrington anyway.' I had to tell my colleagues the news at my leaving party, which could not be called off on such a short notice.

The First Eight Years

The head of personnel was an old army officer and showed no sympathy for our plight. He compensated me for the purchases I had made, but I had to hand over everything, including pieces of lino floor covers, cut to measure, which he must have simply thrown away. In a word, he was a bastard. Of course, Vera was heartbroken. She could not get her old job back and had to move to a less senior one in another department. At least Kellogg's kept her on. We couldn't get our old house back either, and were put up in a family hotel until we managed to buy another house in Hale, Cheshire. Shell paid all our expenses, but there wasn't and couldn't have been any compensation for our time, worries, and discomfort.

István had to go to a new junior school in Altrincham, and later to Altrincham Grammar. We got friendly with a couple, the Bakers, whose two sons went to the same school as István, and Mary Baker kindly offered to look after him during the school holidays. We thought that it was an eminently good solution and only many years later did István tell us that he hated going there. 'Why didn't you tell us at the time?' we asked. 'Because I knew that you had no other choice,' he explained.

The department I was joining was transferred as announced. My new boss, Bill, was a nice man, but not much of a scientist. Fortunately he gave me a free hand and I soon found myself working directly for his boss, who later became the new director of the laboratory, Mr Holliday. He was an ambitious man, a graduate of Oriel College, Oxford, who set himself one goal: to get elected to the Royal Society. His heart was in research, especially into new fields not yet covered by too many establishments. He soon transferred me to the Research Department where I worked on his pet projects.

WHERE IS MY HOME?

Jack Mann, my boss in the Research Department, was a good scientist with a remarkable memory. He is also the only person I've ever known who could sit down and straight away write a long report or a paper for publication that needed no correction later. His main and only hobby was dogs and dog training. Jack was a theoretician, and with me being rather an experimentalist we formed a good team. Later he was sent to a Shell laboratory in America for a year and used to write us long letters about his experience. I used to call them 'Letters from America' after the famous BBC broadcasts of Alistair Cooke. He was a chain smoker, and in meetings you could tell the time by counting the discarded cigarette-ends in his ashtray, one for every fifteen minutes. He had high blood pressure all his life; so much so, that he couldn't get life insurance. Yet he is now ninety and still active in body and mind.

Mr Holliday, Jack, and I had a joint publication in the prestigious journal *Nature*, but unfortunately it was not enough to raise Mr Holliday to the Royal Society. I learned a lot from his management style; he had an impressive ability to get close to people and make them feel important. Once I was taking my mother-in-law to the railway station at Manchester to send her back to London after a visit. Vera and István were both with me, and as we walked along the train I noticed that in the first-class restaurant carriage there sat Mr Holliday. He noticed us too, and by the time we reached the end of the carriage he was down to meet us. He introduced himself, had a pleasant conversation with Granny, who spoke no English, and asked my son what he wanted to do when he grew up.

He also used to arrange regular informal meetings with people in the laboratory, usually inviting us to a nearby pub for a lunch of beer and sandwiches. It was always a mixed lot, including senior scientists as well as assistants, and

The First Eight Years

the discussion was highly intellectual but not necessarily related to our work.

Mr Holliday had a pretty daughter who got married to a young Polish boy. Maybe because of this, one day he invited me and Vera for 'supper' at 8 o'clock in the evening. What was supper? we wondered. In the north of England it is usually a very light meal, typically some cheese and biscuits with coffee. So we had our usual dinner at 6.30 p.m. and arrived at the Hollidays' at eight. We met the rest of the family and were given a glass of sherry, which we expected. However, at about 9 p.m. we were ushered into the next room and were served a full three-course meal. I suppose it was called supper and not dinner as in the south because there was no fish course.

Shell had a small laboratory in London, and Nobel laureate Sir Robert Robinson was in charge of it. I believe Shell kept the lab for him purely as a PR exercise. In return for the facilities, Sir Robert had to provide consultancy to a selection of staff at the various laboratories. Mr Holliday selected five people, myself amongst them. We were lined up in the conference room and Sir Robert came in. One by one we told him a practical problem we were struggling with and Sir Robert listened patiently and replied to each. The trouble was that Sir Robert didn't understand any of the problems we were talking about and we didn't understand his reply.

Mr Holliday's boss and Shell's research coordinator, Mr March, visited our laboratory several times and one time he was introduced to three scientists, including me, for an interview. We were not told as much, but the gossip was that he was looking for someone to go to the USA for a year on an exchange assignment. I remember only one of his questions: 'If you had a choice, would you rather work on a virgin problem or on one on which others had already worked?' My two colleagues both opted for the first, without hesitation. Personally I couldn't see the difference. If there's a problem, it has to be solved, the history is unimportant. 'My wife was a virgin,' I thought. 'That's enough for me.' Eventually none of us was chosen to go to America.

My first serious task was to solve the manufacturing problems of making expanded polystyrene slabs using a monster of a machine. This product was sliced into sheets and used to insulate the roofs and floors of houses. The quality of the slabs was rather poor, especially in the winter, and nobody knew why and what to do about it. I went to the library, read some papers I considered relevant, and carried out some experiments in the laboratory. The result of a few months' work was a clear understanding of each step of the process, which I also published in the journal *British Plastics*. The solution became simple and the problem disappeared.

Mr Holliday was impressed with this work and made me a member of a team tasked with developing a new product, the raw material for the slabs, and with developing our own process to manufacture it. We succeeded, and after the commercial launch of the new product Mr Holiday organised a champagne party for the twenty-five people who had worked on the project. I loved working for Mr Holliday, but unfortunately a few years later his health declined and he retired somewhat ahead of time.

Soon after the champagne party I received a letter from the canteen manager inviting me to dine in the Senior Dining Room. This was how I realised that I had been promoted. Like all young graduates at Shell, I also started in 'job group' five, and after five years I progressed to job group four. This was normal. What was not so normal was that at the start I was already almost thirty years old, while all young British graduates were just twenty-two. Eventually I did progress to job group two, but by then I was too old to be considered for further promotion. I should have escaped right after I received my diploma….

Unlike in the works canteen, in the Senior Dining Room we ate at tables covered with white tablecloths and had waitresses to serve us. We had a cooked three-course meal and we could help ourselves to cheese as well. I especially liked the blue Stilton, which was brought in as a full truckle, from which we had to scoop out the middle with a spoon. While I obviously enjoyed the luxury, I now know that it was wrong to separate the workers from their bosses. A single canteen would have improved communication between them, leading to a better relationship. Maybe as an additional reward, Mr Holliday sent me to a very prestigious conference of polymer scientists held yearly at Mortonhampstead in Devon. Attendance was by invitation only, but of course his request to invite me was granted. I arrived with my boss, his wife, the head of the department, Dr Howard, and his wife. I met there, amongst others, Gerry McCrum, an Oxford don. We had a private discussion, and I mentioned to him my plans for future research. He liked them and suggested that I come to Oxford for, as I understood, a further discussion. On my return to Carrington I was busy with my work when one day I had a phone call from Gerry:

'When are you coming?'

'I haven't made any definite plans yet.'

'Would it help if my professor wrote a letter to your director?'

I replied a little offended by the suggestion: 'No need for that! For a day-trip to Oxford I don't need such powerful help, I can arrange it any time.'

'But it's not for just a day, it's for two years!'

'What do you mean?'
'Have you got a PhD?'
'No,' I had to reply.
'Do you want one?'

I had ten seconds' thinking time and said yes. An important consideration in my decision was that in Oxford I could, in principle, complete a DPhil in two years if I studied full-time. The alternative would have been to have an evening course lasting several years. Mr Holliday was most helpful. He told me to consider one college only: Balliol, because of its reputation for very high academic standards, so I applied and they accepted me. He arranged for me a two-year leave of absence without pay, during which time Shell continued to pay my company- and state-pension contribution. I also got an invitation to visit the laboratory once a month to discuss my work, which was useful to them as manufacturers of resins. For this consultancy I was paid £20. Gerry managed to get a grant for me from the Ministry of Aviation, because I was going to work on a project related to the development of Concorde.

3
Getting a DPhil.

I WAS excited at the chance of getting a doctorate, and, what was more, from Oxford. I had dreamed about my son going to study there, but had never imagined myself doing it. Any doubt about my abilities were swept away by the fact that my director and my would-be doctoral supervisor had confidence in me. I felt certain that this was the opportunity of a lifetime, one which would never be repeated and which I had to grab with both hands.

We let our house in Hale and rented a flat in a newly built apartment house in Oxford. We enrolled István at Oxford Grammar. Vera gave up her job at Kellogg's and felt very miserable. Finally we packed everything into the car and drove down to Oxford. We had a big rubber tree and placed it in the front seat, between Vera's knees. She cried for almost the full three-and-a-half-hour journey. She felt uprooted going into the unknown, and was already missing her friends and especially her job. The next time Vera cried was when we were returning to Hale.

As soon as we arrived, Vera got a part-time job at a Coca-Cola bottling plant as the director's secretary. He was an older and very charming man who lived with his wife in a beautiful, old house. He looked after Vera as though she were his daughter and regularly encouraged her to drink one of their products, Fanta, to get more energy. The only trouble was that he assumed Vera could write in English shorthand, and one day he just started to dictate a letter. Vera used her best Hungarian shorthand, but after that she quickly had to take a few lessons from a teacher.

Our income had been reduced by half, and we had to start life in Oxford rather sombrely, having lunch at the cafeteria in Woolworths and buying windfall apples at the cattle market. We couldn't afford to buy expensive meat, so occasionally Vera bought a pig's head. She asked the butcher: 'Could you please remove the eyes, they're looking at me.' The butcher obliged, but Vera was not yet satisfied: 'Would you please also remove its teeth as well?'

'Madam,' said the man, 'I'm a butcher, not a dentist!' But he did as she asked.

We appointed a friend of ours as an agent to manage our house in Hale, but we still had a lot of trouble with our tenants. Once a budding pop-group rented it, but didn't pay the rent. I used to call their bank but, of course, they referred me to their clients. Later a businessman rented it, also without paying. When I phoned him, he said that his company was responsible for the rent, not him. However, we found out that he was using our house as a love nest for two girls from the Caribbean. They were probably illegal immigrants, because after I talked to them on the telephone and threatened them with the police if they didn't pay the rent, they quickly disappeared.

I became a member of Balliol, a college with a reputation for excellent academic achievement. Because the college was high on the list for many applicants they could select from the best, and because of their fame they had no problem in attracting excellent teaching staff (known as 'Fellows'). The college was 700 years old, one of the very oldest in Oxford. I had no tutor, only a supervisor, Gerry McCrum, who was a Fellow of Hertford College and a lecturer at the Department of Engineering Science. Like everybody else, I had to have a moral tutor from my college as well. He was supposed to look after all the personal problems of his students, but he was younger than me and his only tutoring of me consisted of a lunch-party organised every term at a restaurant.

Gerry was a physicist and specialised in polymer physics. He was a short, middle-aged man, and had just bought a beautiful, new car with the money he had received as an

Getting a D.Phil

expert witness in a US case involving a disputed patent. His American wife was writing cookery books. They had two children, a beautiful house in Summertown, and did a lot of entertaining. Alas, they later divorced.

I knew that I had no time to waste if I wanted to stay for two years only, so I was eager to start working as soon as possible. The subject of polymer physics was not entirely unknown to me, but I underestimated the knowledge of the theoretical background I needed. When my supervisor talked about the work he spat out expressions I only vaguely understood. I was the oldest student and was surrounded by brilliant, young men talking about their research, which I couldn't always follow. The whole academic atmosphere was so different from industry that it really scared me. What had I got myself into? My director and supervisor were wrong after all! For weeks I had nightmares, contemplating quitting with a good excuse rather than wait for the inevitable humiliation. But when I started my experiments, and when I got my teeth into practical problems I understood and managed to solve them, things started to improve. I also worked harder and was better organised than most of my younger colleagues. After a month or two I felt on the top of the world, and my inferiority complex vanished.

At the end of each term, like every other student I also appeared in front of the Master and was told if my work was satisfactory or not. Because I already had a university degree I was considered a mature student, and the information had to come from my supervisor, Gerry. Once it so happened that the Master read out to me a report written for another student, who had been to see him just before me. It was a good report, so I said nothing, wondering what the next student would think when my report was read out to him in turn. It was obvious that the process was meaningless, but this was Oxford, that bastion of tradition.

WHERE IS MY HOME?

We were quite friendly with the deputy master, Mr Meiggs, who was also the warden of an extension to the college. When he retired at the age of seventy, he told us his motto: 'Life begins at seventy.' At the time we smiled, but now I understand him.

Meiggs was a Fellow in Ancient History and occasionally went on cruises and lectured to rich American tourists as the ship passed by famous sites. He and the Fellow in Physics, Heinrich Kuhn, were not called 'doctors' because their PhD hadn't been awarded by a university with a college structure. There were only three such universities: Oxford, Cambridge, and Dublin. They believed in the saying, attributed to Kipling, that 'a cauliflower is a cabbage with a college education.' Oxford calls the degree a DPhil rather than a PhD, I suppose just to be different.

I had a laboratory which I shared with two other students, also working for their DPhil and led by the same supervisor. Another room next door was air-conditioned and housed the departmental computers. They were in huge cabinets, all using old fashioned radio valves. I do not know for sure, but I think that today the small laptop I have used to write this book can do more than all those cabinets put together.

I considered the tuition fee I had to pay to the college exorbitant, but the fellows enjoyed a very good life and somebody had to pay for it. We had a Junior Common Room for the undergraduates and a Senior Common Room for the students who, like me, already had a degree. This SCR was a new extension and a gift of the King of Norway, who had studied at Balliol. Indeed there were many famous people, ex-prime ministers, and so on who had been educated at Balliol. We also had a canteen, and later I would eat my lunch there. Twice I was invited to dine at High Table with my supervisor at Hertford College. This was a relatively

Getting a D.Phil

poor college like Balliol, quite unlike St. John's, which was the richest in Oxford. The reason for the difference was that St. John's had invested its original endowment in land and now owned vast areas of highly valuable real estate. Balliol meanwhile had invested in coal mines, which had lost value over the years. Still, the food and drink at High Table in Hertford were a feast to remember. After the meal, we moved into another room to drink a choice of claret or port and smoke a cigar. We sat at a round table and the bottles were passed from person to person. Fortunately, smoking was not compulsory.

Because I was a member of a college, I could participate in all sorts of cultural and social activities, often together with Vera. I also met many brilliant and interesting people. One evening we attended a piano recital at Balliol given by Moura Lympany, a famous concert pianist. She was persuaded to perform for us by Ted Heath, the former prime minister, who was also a Balliol old boy and was known for his love of classical music. Once, he even conducted the London Symphony Orchestra at the Albert Hall. He was present at the recital, shaking hands with lots of people. On another occasion I attended a talk given by the famous Hungarian-born physicist Professor Polányi. The title of his talk was 'Tacit Knowledge', and he gave as an example the fact that we can't scientifically describe a face, but we still instantly recognise it. During questions I suggested that one day it might become possible to accurately describe it as well. He was saddened by my comment, and admitted that it was indeed a serious danger to his theory. As it happens, with digital technology we have already come rather close to this position. In the interval I had a short talk with him, and he liked the fact that this difficult point was raised by another ex-Hungarian scientist.

WHERE IS MY HOME?

My research work was sponsored by the Ministry of Aviation. This was a time when Concorde was being developed, and almost the whole Engineering Department was working on various parts of the project. An aerial had to protrude from the nose of the aeroplane, and it had to be insulated from the body by a non-conductive plastic material. The trouble was that, because of its high speed, the nose temperature reached up to 400°C, and no known plastic could stand up to this. I had to work closely with chemists from the Royal Aircraft Establishment at Farnborough, who used ingenious technology and developed new experimental polymers for me to evaluate. I had to test them and advise them on the relationship between chemical structure and physical properties. Based on my advice, they changed the composition until they got it right. Before I could take any measurements I had to develop my instrument, which was not commercially available. Besides testing the samples from Farnborough, I also tested several commercially-available, so-called 'engineering polymers' to get a better understanding of the relationship between structure and thermal behaviour. To complete the work, I also prepared and tested several epoxy resins, systematically varying their chemical structure. These resins were made of two components, like the epoxy-resin glues used today, and had to be mixed in a prescribed ratio. I had to work with several electronic instruments new to me, and one day I managed to burn out one of them. It had to be repaired, but fortunately I didn't have to pay for it. I suppose the cause of the trouble was that I am rather quick in doing things and use too little time to think about it first. Unfortunately this character trait is still with me.

Every three months a delegation came from Farnborough to discuss my results, and after the discussion Gerry would take us all out to dinner at his college. They were most

Getting a D.Phil

satisfied with my work, and, as we all know, Concorde proved to be a successful aeroplane at supersonic speeds. What's more important, I got my DPhil.

I made regular visits to Shell's laboratories, informing them of my findings. The instrument and the technique were also useful to chemists working on various industrial polymers. However, I don't think that they made any use of my results, as it hadn't been invented by them. Once I also went to Basel, to talk to scientists at Ciba-Geigy. They were competitors of Shell, but I had been doing this work on behalf of Oxford University. Ciba-Geigy had an excellent reputation amongst the scientific community, especially Professor Batzer, who had numerous publications on the topic I was working on. I was received by him and by one of his assistants. To start with, I complimented him by saying that I felt that I was 'bringing coals to Newcastle'. I made a short presentation of my results, linking the physical properties of the resins to their chemical structure. At first Batzer didn't believe me, but when I gave a more detailed account of my experiments he backed down. Eventually he was very pleased with the information he received from me. The equipment they had been using had suffered from the same problems I had had, but had remedied, on mine. When I explained what I did and showed them my results, they were most impressed. At the end Batzer asked me if I would allow him to make a photocopy of one of my sheets. Since by the nature of the contract between the university and Farnborough all the work I did was publishable, I gave my permission and he came back not only with my original, but also an envelope containing 100 Swiss francs. The money enabled me to travel the next day up to the 3,000m-high Jungfrau on a cog railway.

WHERE IS MY HOME?

I met many interesting people at Oxford, and not just from Balliol, and we kept in contact with several of them long after our return to Manchester. At the university the most important person for me was my supervisor, Gerry. He was a physicist and didn't understand much of the chemistry I was working with. Once, he asked me to prepare for him two components which he could mix in class to demonstrate their hardening into a more or less single molecule (like an epoxy glue). I did it using exact ratios, without any excess of either component, to ensure a complete reaction. He didn't have the patience to empty the entire contents of one of the containers into the other. The result was a delayed reaction, and the demonstration failed. He was not amused, and deposited the glass container at the concierge and told me to pick it up sometime. In the meantime the reaction progressed and accelerated, and, at a certain, unannounced moment, the single molecule was formed, a process accompanied by the formation of a fair amount of heat and smoke as well. The concierge had no idea what it was and almost called the fire brigade!

One time, Gerry invited me and Vera for dinner together with another couple. He was a lecturer specialising in a remote language nobody spoke any more. While eating chicken Kiev, he asked me bluntly what I thought of his topic: did I think the study of such a remote language justified a chair at Oxford ? Equally bluntly, I said 'no'. I was not against it in principle, but I considered it a question of choice: in an ideal world with unlimited resources I would have said 'yes'. But this is not an ideal world, and if it is a question of spending money on medical research *or* on such an extravagance, I would choose the former.

The next person closest to us was a Canadian postdoctoral fellow, Layton M. He had a great deal of theoretical knowledge, and a fair amount of practical ability as well,

Getting a D.Phil

and he was very much interested in cooking and eating. Vera admired with some envy his stainless-steel, copper-bottomed pots and pans and other utensils. Later he married his girlfriend and we were invited to Cambridge to the wedding. When he left Oxford, he got a job as a lecturer at the University of Exeter, and in this capacity he was later to be my external examiner. We still see each other occasionally. We also became rather friendly with a very nice Belgian couple with two young children. They used to speak Dutch amongst themselves in our presence, which was very annoying, and to show our disapproval we started to speak Hungarian. We always thought of them as the ideal couple, but unfortunately we later learned that the wife had decided that she was a lesbian. She left her husband taking the children with her, and the husband went to Holland to teach Aristotelian philosophy at the University of Utrecht. He stayed with us for a few weeks until he found permanent accommodation. We were friendly with another senior student, Dudley, also a member of Balliol, studying PPE (Philosophy, Politics and Economics). He was a short boy, but fell in love with a tall, slim, Canadian girl. They decided to marry, and a date was set. We too were invited, but on the evening prior to the occasion someone pushed a note under our front door. It simply read '…the wedding will not take place as announced.' We still don't know the reason why. All we know is that that he never married. He wrote several books on economics, including a study of the Australian economy utilising lots of research and statistics. Dudley became a Professor of Economics first at Ashton, then in Australia. He is now a retired Emeritus Professor, and we still keep in contact. Occasionally, when in Europe, he visits us. Dudley is also an excellent cook, and I wonder if it is pure coincidence that most of our friends are good cooks.

WHERE IS MY HOME?

At the department of Engineering Science worked a Polish lecturer, who after several years was still working on his DPhil. He liked me because I was Hungarian and, like most Poles, disliked the Czechs. He told me how much Polish people admired the Hungarian revolution, and told me a Polish joke: 'The Hungarians behaved as the Poles should have done, the Poles behaved as the Czechs, and the Czechs behaved, as usual, like cowards.' He supervised an Indian boy, Arvin, also working for his DPhil, who was about to test his theory on heat transfer. He made his equipment and started his measurements, but, to his horror, they didn't prove his theory. Arvin's greatest asset was his knowledge of cooking an excellent curry. One time, we organised a party in our flat. Arvin was doing the cooking and we were sitting around our bed, using it as a dining table. When everybody was served, Arvin asked permission from Vera to eat as he would at home. Permission granted, he sat down on the floor and ate the remains from the pot using three of his fingers. He remarked that some stupid European tourists think that eating with their hand means using the whole hand. Not so: Indian etiquette required using the ends of three fingers only. And, of course, only the right hand should be used for eating, while the left must be reserved for various 'dirty jobs'.

A post-graduate chemistry student from Pakistan, Ishaqu, was also a member of Balliol. He too invited us to his home for a curry, which was the hottest meal I have ever had. When I grasped for the tomato salad to quench the fire in my mouth, I was shocked to find that the tomato had been stuffed with green chilli pepper before being sliced and dressed. Ishaqu fell in love with a girl from the Sudan, but, as luck would have it, the girl was not Muslim but Coptic. Of course his family was against the marriage and sent his uncle to bring him to his senses. When this

Getting a D.Phil

didn't work, they insisted that he return home for a 'visit'. He told us sadly that he knew why he was being invited back home—to marry someone his family had chosen for him. He knew it, but yet he went. This was at the end of our stay and we lost contact, but I have heard that he is now teaching chemistry in Saudi Arabia, very likely married to one of his cousins.

Ishaqu was also friendly with Arvin, the Indian boy, and when the war between their two countries started they both felt embarrassed. At first they didn't know how to approach the other, but they soon realised that the war had nothing to do with them and with their friendship. They just continued as if nothing has happened.

Oxford was a truly cosmopolitan town, and there were several mixed marriages. Aslam came from Pakistan, but he had grown up in East Africa. He was Muslim, but not religious, and married Annie, a Catholic girl from Austria. One colleague of my wife was married to a man from Persia. Another girl had a boyfriend from India, and when they came to us for supper we were concerned about what to put in the sandwiches: a Hindu wouldn't eat beef, a Muslim must not eat pork. He turned out to be a faithful Roman Catholic, and because it was a Friday he didn't eat any meat at all.

An Egyptian couple lived in the same block of flats as us, and we visited each other a few times. He also worked at the Department of Engineering, and invited us for dinner once. They had an Egyptian maid who cooked the food, which was rather spicy but not very hot. We went with them one time to a concert in the library of Blenheim Palace. This was a special occasion: ladies had to wear party dresses and gentlemen smoking jackets.

An Irish architect and his wife also lived in the same block of flats. They were very much concerned about

WHERE IS MY HOME?

Going to Blenheim

preserving the character of Oxford, which they thought was in danger due to over-crowding. When they invited us round, he taught me how to drink whiskey. 'After each glass of whiskey you have to drink a large glass of water,' he said. It worked, and we almost finished the bottle without becoming tipsy. His wife shared a bottle of white vine with Vera without drinking water. According to English custom, there was nothing to eat, not even some crisps.

Another neighbour was a lecturer in zoology and once took us to the countryside to observe some wild otters. We had to get up rather early, went to the desired spot, and waited quietly for hours without seeing one. He gave a few stick insects to István, who kept them in a jar and fed them with fresh leaves. A brilliant young American, Richard P., came to Oxford and lectured on economics. Because he wanted to study planned economics in Hungary, he took a few lessons in the Hungarian language from Vera. I tried to persuade him to study a more deserving subject than a planned economy, but without success.

Getting a D.Phil

We met a very nice couple from Sri Lanka, and one evening they invited me and my wife and an English couple for dinner. I like curry, so I was looking forward to the food, which was, indeed, delicious. They served a huge portion, and it took some time, but we managed to clear our plates. Our host immediately offered another helping, and insisted on emptying the whole pot. To our surprise, as soon as we had finished eating our Sri Lankan hostess went to the kitchen and returned with another pot. Well, I like curry, but I can tell you that I struggled to consume the third helping. Finally, the second pot too was empty, and we felt rather proud of our achievement. To our great relief, no more curry was brought in. We had a very pleasant evening, and went home rather late. On the way home I said to Vera: 'You know that I like curry, but I wouldn't mind if you didn't cook any for a very long time.' Next morning we were woken by the doorbell. It was our Sri Lankan hostess, and guess what she had brought us: a large pot of curry! I just had to tell this to our English friends with whom we had spent the evening. I phoned and started telling the story, when he interrupted me. 'Please hang on for a second; someone's at the door....' After this I didn't have to explain anything. What we didn't know was that in Sri Lanka the housewife should always cook and serve so much food that some is left uneaten by the guests. In other words, while we thought that we were being very polite by cleaning our plates, we were, in fact, being very rude. As soon as we had left, the husband had scolded his wife and sent her off to cook more food and so save the honour of the family.

We met a Hungarian student married to an English girl, who invited us for dinner. He wanted to show off his wife's ability to cook an authentic Hungarian goulash. What made this even more remarkable was the fact that his wife was a vegetarian.

WHERE IS MY HOME?

István benefited a lot from Oxford's intellectual environment. He was present at the dinner table each time we had guests, and occasionally he too was invited when we visited friends. He always participated in the discussion, and I was rather proud of him.

I met a Russian post-doctoral student who was working in the Department of Engineering Science, where most people on the Concorde project worked. The thought occurred to me that he might be an industrial spy, but after talking to him I was convinced that he was not. Boris lived in a separate college building reserved for advanced students, but he too had to observe the rules. There were to be no female visitors after 11pm, when the big, strong door of the building was closed. All students had to be in by this time, and all visitors gone. If the 'scouts' (as the college servants were called) found anybody absent, or any stranger in the room of a student, they had to report it to the Proctor. The most likely result of this was that the student would be 'sent down', i.e. expelled from the college, which meant automatic expulsion from the university as well. Another medieval rule of the university was that during term students were not allowed to leave the boundaries of the city of Oxford without the Proctor's permission. Because Boris couldn't think of a good excuse, he never asked for permission, and never saw that beautiful stretch of countryside called the Cotswolds, with their stone buildings and quaint pubs, which are so close to the city. He didn't even dare go to London in case someone saw him at the station or on the train. He was sure that he was being specially watched by the British secret service.

On his arrival in college, other students explained such rules to him. They also showed him the 'steps' as they were called, which consisted simply of a loose brick in one wall

Getting a D.Phil

of the college and a piece of stone placed against the inside face. Its purpose was to allow any student coming home late to climb in without exposing himself to the authorities. It was useful to know the exact position of the step, because the stone wall was rather high and trying to climb it at any other place might have resulted in a nasty accident. Worse still, the intruder would certainly have been noticed and the disciplinary procedure would have been unavoidable. For latecomers it was either the step or nothing at all. It was common knowledge that every college had such a spot, but the authorities turned a blind eye. Who after all would take responsibility for having changed a centuries-old tradition? Some of the fellows might have used it themselves while they were studying for their degree many years ago.

I met Boris for the first time in the Senior Common Room, where was always coffee, tea, and a decanter of sherry to hand. Anyone taking a glass would have only to sign his name in the book provided and the price would be added to his end of term bill. Whenever a student had a second glass, he had to insert an extra stroke in the book after his name. The system assumed honesty, but it could also have been misused. It made cash and pre-purchased tickets unnecessary. The first time Boris wanted to make use of these facilities, he didn't know how the system worked. He was too shy to ask, and decided instead to wait and observe how others were coping with it. I had just refilled my glass with a second measure of sherry and put a stroke in the book after my name. Boris, who had seen me drawing the stroke only, took a glass, filled it, and innocently put yet another stroke after my name. I didn't say a word, thinking that there was a time when I was a newcomer in England and, anyway, I could easily afford to treat him to a glass of sherry. I don't know who explained the correct procedure to him, but one day he came to my laboratory bringing a bottle of sherry as a peace offering. In return I invited him for dinner. 'So this is authentic Hungarian goulash?' he asked my wife after consuming a second helping.

'It is,' she answered, 'and you can have still more.'

'No, no, I already had too much,' he protested. 'But I couldn't resist it after eating English food for the past three months. Salt and pepper seem to be the only spices they know in this country.'

'You're right, of course,' I admitted with some satisfaction. 'But if you want to taste real English cooking at its best, you should not do it in college, but at the Trout Inn. It's a bit expensive, but the food is superb.'

'I can't afford that, not from my allowance,' said Boris with a big sigh. 'It'll be different when I get a job at the Physical Research Institute in Moscow. There'll be more opportunity to travel, and I'll get a better allowance. Until now, I didn't think that I could get a job in Moscow, but with a successful year at Oxford all doors will be open for me.'

'So you can relax now, you've made it….'

'Not quite, I still have to watch my step, I can't afford any mishaps.'

'What on earth do you mean? What could possibly go wrong?'

'There are so many strange rules here, you know.'

'Nobody keeps all those rules, especially not the advanced students.'

'I've made up my mind to obey all of them while I'm in Oxford. Just imagine what'll happen if I'm expelled and arrive back in Minsk before my time's up? What a shame it would be!'

'Presumably your whole career would also be ruined,' I admitted. 'Would you have to forget about Moscow as well?' I didn't say it, but I was sure that his whole family

Getting a D.Phil

would also be made to suffer for his sins. Maybe he'd done it on purpose, it would be alleged. Maybe it was the influence of the CIA, so as to bring shame on the Soviet Union? Maybe he'd become a spy? I knew how communist societies worked. Boris could almost read my mind, because he said: 'You know, this must be the real reason why they didn't allow my wife and daughter to come with me. I said to the Party Secretary "a year is a long time, Yury Alexandrovits, and I could concentrate better on my work if I had my family with me." "Sure," he'd said, "if there are no problems." "What problems do you mean?" I'd asked. "Well, just suppose your child got ill in a strange, capitalist country. That would worry you a lot comrade, wouldn't it?" And that was the end of the conversation,' said Boris, discreetly omitting any reference to the possible temptation of staying in the West. I only nodded my head in understanding. I could imagine that conversation very well, but I didn't want to embarrass my guest any further. To change the subject, I asked him if he was interested in seeing my collection of Hungarian stamps. He was.

There is a lot of history in a stamp collection. Hungarian stamps started out with a picture of the Austrian Habsburg emperor, followed by pictures of the Hungarian Parliament. These stamps also had *Magyar Királyi Posta*, 'Hungarian Royal Post', printed upon them. After the First World War, for a short period there was communist rule and the stamps were overprinted with the word *Köztársaság*, 'Republic', and the word for 'Royal' also disappeared and simply became 'Hungarian Post.' The word for 'Royal' came back with the arrival of a regent, Admiral Horthy, in 1920. Just before the Second World War, parts of old Hungary were returned and this was clearly marked on some stamps as well. Later, there were an abundance of stamps issued by the communist regime, merely as a way to earn more money. I stopped actively collecting stamps issued after 1945, but if I happened upon one I put it into my album.

'Hey, this is Stalin!' exclaimed Boris looking at the familiar face. 'He wasn't Hungarian! Why's he on a Hungarian stamp?' I found it strange that he was surprised at this, since it was not only on stamps that we put the picture of the beloved leader of the Soviet Union. Hungary, and all the other East European countries, were full of statues of him as well. But by now the year was 1965, Khrushchev was in power, and Stalin was not only dead but also out of favour even in Russia. Strangely, it was up to me to explain to Boris the facts of communist history.

Boris had taken to the academic life in Oxford like a duck to water. He worked long hours, quietly, keeping to all the rules with an iron will, motivated by a hope in a brighter future. He didn't frequent the popular places, like the famous Trout Inn, where on a Sunday morning students drank beer at the side of the lock, watching the fish and the ducks and the occasional swan. He worked either in the Radcliffe Science Library or in his laboratory, leaving these only to return to his college. The one time he ever got a little merry was when he received a parcel from a member of a visiting Russian trade delegation. It contained a tin of real caviar and a bottle of vodka, sent to him by his wife. He decided to share it with me and also invited both his supervisor and his moral tutor to the party. Like everybody else, he too had to have a supervisor and a moral tutor. The fact that Boris was a married man with a family, while his moral tutor was a young bachelor, was not considered relevant to his necessity. This was the first time I had tasted real caviar, and I found it rather too salty.

As the end of his year at Oxford was approaching, Boris relaxed a little. He was happy with the knowledge and information he had amassed and was sure he would become

Getting a D.Phil

indispensable in Moscow. His English too had improved considerably, and he could look forward to tours abroad in due course. So, for the first time, he was seriously considering an invitation from his moral tutor to go with him to see the beautiful Cotswolds as a farewell act to his study in Oxford. Boris decided to consult me on the matter.

'How can I accept this invitation when it'll take me outside the limits of the city?'

'You must understand Boris, this rule isn't meant for you. It's to ensure that undergraduate students do their work in Oxford. Otherwise someone might enrol, go away, and present himself for the examination only. This would defeat the college and tutorial system.'

'Shouldn't I ask permission from the Proctor?'

'No! That'd be ridiculous. You're not even receiving a degree; this student status is only a formality for you.'

'And what about being late back to college? Can I get in late without any repercussions?'

'The college is like a hotel, it has its own rules. It wouldn't be practical to have any exceptions. But you know where the step is, don't you? That's what it's for.' This argument seemed to put his mind at rest, and he accepted the lift from his tutor. Off they went, first to the Swan Inn at Burford, then to the King's Arms, and finally to the Hare & Hounds. In spite of the large quantity of beer consumed they both remained sober and decided that it was time to return home. It was just after 10pm, so there was plenty of time to get back to the college before the gates closed. Unfortunately, just before Witney they had a flat tyre. Boris considered hitchhiking back to Oxford, but decided that it wouldn't be right to leave his companion alone to deal with the emergency. The job took longer than expected, and they found the college gate had just closed. 'Do you know where the step is?' asked his tutor, who lived in private lodgings.

WHERE IS MY HOME?

'Sure, I know' answered Boris confidently.

'Then see you tomorrow!' said the tutor, and without waiting for a reply he drove away. Boris walked slowly towards the spot, marked clearly by a loose brick. He found it and removed the brick carefully to create a foothold. The brick was still in his hand when suddenly he found himself confronted by a policeman.

'Good evening sir,' said the policeman in his official voice. He was tall, like all British policemen were, wearing his typical helmet and walking and talking slowly, but emphasising each word as if they could all have been interpreted differently. He was obviously trained to be precise, and to avoid all misunderstandings. Boris was small, in comparison, not very sporty either, and saw no hope in running away. He blamed himself for not looking around more carefully before removing that brick. He should have known that he was being watched by the British. Now he had been caught red-handed, and had betrayed the trust of this country. What's more, he was holding a brick in his hand and could have been mistaken for a hooligan.

'Good evening,' he replied, and knew at once that he made another big mistake. From his accent the policeman could immediately tell his background even if he hadn't known already. This could lead to an international incident, Boris thought, and probably a recall of respective ambassadors. Who could say, it might even go down as the start of the Third World War. The policeman seem to have noticed his hesitation and waited a long time.

'Well now, sir,' he said finally in a patient voice. 'Can you climb it by yourself, or do you want me to give you a hand?'

When Boris' term had finished and he had to return home, he organised a farewell party offering, once again, real caviar and vodka. I was invited, and this became the second time I tasted real caviar. It still tasted salty, but I

86

Getting a D.Phil

asked and got his permission to take a small sample back home for Vera and István.

If you belonged to a college, life in Oxford was excellent. We had plenty of social contacts and in spite of the loss of income we were eating out more and enjoyed life. The greatest attraction for me though was the River Cherwell, where we could punt. This meant pushing the punt with a long pole, and after each push using the same pole to steer. One time I let István do the punting but the pole got stuck in the mud. He decided to hang on to the pole instead of the boat, and fell into the water. Fortunately it was a warm day. More serious boating took place on the River Thames, which in Oxford is called the Isis. In the spring it was customary just to sit at the club-house of one's college and watch the boats while eating strawberries and cream. During my time there, Oxford won the famous boat race against Cambridge.

Oxford is such a beautiful town that several of our friends decided to visit us. If they came from Manchester, we always asked them to bring us some drinking water, because the local water tasted terrible. Hungarian guests had to bring some fresh paprika, which was not available anywhere in England. We took our guests on a conducted tour of the colleges and their gardens. My favourite was New College, where in the hall we could see a board with the names of all the old boys who had died as soldiers during the Second World War. Next to it was a separate board with the name of a single German, also an old boy, who had died for his country in the same war. This could only happen in England.

Once every two years each college organised a commemorative ball. It was a tremendous occasion of eating, drinking, and dancing throughout the night. For breakfast they served bacon and eggs with champagne. Once we attended a concert in the Sheldonian Theatre given by Yehudi Menuhin. I don't know which was more impressive, the beautiful interior of the building or the music. Perhaps it was just the general atmosphere. Next day there was an article about the concert in one of the better newspapers. To our surprise, or even horror, it criticised Yehudi Menuhin, accusing him of occasionally having hit a bad note. Why had the audience applauded so much? Because nobody but the writer could detect a note half a pitch too low, was his less-than-modest suggestion.

You might be wondering how I managed to present my Hungarian university degree to the college, when I had left it in Hungary in 1956. Well, this is how. In Hungary, between 1950 and 1956 we had had very little money in spite of the fact that I had been working as a graduate chemist and my wife as a qualified statistician. The salary had been enough to live on as accommodation was cheap, while food—what was available—was also reasonably priced, but it had been a major undertaking to buy any item of clothing. We had had to save for several months to buy a pair of shoes or a new shirt, and when I needed a new winter coat we had had to save for it over two years. The first year, we had saved enough to buy the material. In Hungary there were no shops where you could buy good quality, ready-to-wear clothing; on the other hand, tailors were cheap and abundant. The second year, we had had enough money to have the coat made. It had been a real beauty; I had never before owned such a luxurious garment. This had been in the year 1956.

I decided not to attempt to escape to the West wearing my new winter coat. If we were caught and returned, I might arrive with a torn and ruined coat and it would take me another two years to get a new one. It would have broken my

Getting a D.Phil

heart. If we succeeded in our attempt, we would be refugees and could walk around in my old coat. If I got a job, we would be able to buy a new one. The plan worked, and I arrived in Austria wearing my old coat, which was indeed much the worse for the journey. It had a sheepskin lining, made of small pieces sown together. It had started to come apart at several seams. Arriving in England a few months later, we realised that the climate was much less harsh than what we had expected, given its geographical position. We knew nothing of the effect of the Gulf Stream. In England people wore raincoats only, even during winter, and I would have looked ridiculous in that old coat of mine, which I promptly discarded in the dustbin. When my mother-in-law got permission to leave Hungary and come to England, she was allowed to take with her a limited amount of goods only, mainly her old, used, personal belongings. I travelled to Dover to meet her and I was most surprised to see her arriving in my new winter coat which I had left behind. She had given up her right to wear her own winter coat and thought to do me a great favour by bringing mine out. I had to thank her and buy for her another coat, but of course in the end I never wore mine, because it was much too heavy and warm. Its style, too, with those large, military lapels, looked distinctively East European.

About five years later a friend and old colleague of mine managed to get a passport and visited us. He brought us some Hungarian paprika, a goose liver cooked in its own fat, Hungarian salami, and a few tubes of goulash paste. But he also brought me something very useful, my original university diploma. I hadn't needed this to get a job, but when I enrolled in Oxford for my DPhil they did indeed ask for it. In return, I gave him the coat.

WHERE IS MY HOME?

According to the rules of the university, I had to spend a minimum of two years (six terms) in residence, but had seven years to write and present my thesis. Writing could be done at home, but one is not allowed to refer to any experiment not carried out in Oxford. Being aware of this rule I considered that my priority was to carry out as many experiments as possible during those two years. This was very much against the standard practice at Oxford, not to mention the advice of my supervisor.

'The right thing to do,' he said to me more as a request than as advice, 'is to spend most of your time constructing a theory, then do a few experiments to prove it.' But what if I couldn't prove it? I would have wasted two years of my life. Fortunately I kept good records of my experiments, and I made sure that I was taking with me everything necessary to write my thesis. We packed our personal belongings, I borrowed a minivan from Shell, and we left Oxford in September of 1966 and returned to our house in Manchester after just one year and eleven months away. I returned to work at Shell, finished writing my thesis, and they helped me to type and print it (154 pages in all, with nine pages of references). As a motto, I put on the first page a quotation from Newton: 'For the best and safest method of philosophising seems to me, first diligently to investigate the properties of things and establish them by experiment, and then to seek hypotheses to explain them....' If it was good enough for Newton, I thought, it should be good enough for me.

When I analysed my experimental results, I was able to draw several conclusions, some of them practical, but some of them also theoretically interesting. Later I turned them into five publications in learned papers. I submitted my thesis in April of 1967 and took my *viva voce* examination in June. My internal examiner was a lecturer of organic

Getting a D.Phil

chemistry and this worried me at first, because my general theoretical knowledge of the subject was dated to say the least. But this was not an exam for an undergraduate, and in defending a thesis they were supposed to ask relevant questions only. Besides, he knew nothing about my subject of polymer physics. My external examiner was Layton. The *viva* was in theory supposed to be open to any past and present member of the university, but, as usual, nobody else came. It lasted about an hour, and I was at ease right from the start. Layton did his best to be difficult and concentrated his questions on a few points where we had had disagreements in the past. The internal examiner though was very polite and didn't ask a single difficult question. After the exam I met Layton in the evening and asked him of the result. He told me that the internal examiner was very satisfied with my performance. 'There's no doubt about this at all,' he had said to Layton.

'Have I passed?' I pressed him.

'Unless you run over the vice-chancellor with your car tonight, you have,' he said. 'You realise that part of the fee you had to pay is going to a most worthy cause?' He was referring, of course, to his own pocket.

I got my leave to apply for the degree of DPhil, which I promptly did. After paying the appropriate fee, I was invited to the degree ceremony, which was held in the Sheldonian Theatre. I had to borrow from the concierge of the college a special gown for doctors of the University of Oxford, and I processed in with the other graduates. All colleges presented their BA students to the vice-chancellor one group at a time. DPhil students on the other hand were presented one by one. We shook hands with the vice-chancellor and promptly took our places in seats reserved for doctors of the university. It was a uniquely pleasant feeling. After the ceremony, the three of us had an evening meal at the most famous Oxford restaurant, The Elizabeth, which sadly is no more. I had moussaka, the cheapest dish, and either from the fat or more probably from the excitement I was sick on the premises. Just like after I had received my diploma in chemistry in Hungary, I became rather big-headed. I thought that when I returned to Shell I would immediately be put in charge of a research department. But it didn't happen, as I shall soon explain.

Looking back on our time in Oxford we have to confess that, in spite of some financial hardship, it was the most beautiful two years of our lives. We loved the atmosphere, enjoyed meeting interesting people, and loved boating on the river. Because of the international community we felt less foreign than we had in Manchester. The feeling that it was an artificial life, full of snobbery, has long faded away.

Vera, the author, and István outside Oxford's Sheldonian Theatre

4
The last years in England.

RETURNING from Oxford, we found that our troublesome tenants had already left and our house in Hale was in a reasonable condition, so we could move in at once. Our neighbours were all delighted, perhaps not so much with us but with the quiet, normal life returning to the Avenue. Vera couldn't return to Kellogg's, and eventually got a new job at Beechams, the pharmaceutical company, as secretary to the marketing manager. We soon settled down to a life which, by now, was well known to us. We developed a routine: on Friday evenings we used to have fish and chips, wrapped in newspaper of course, which we bought in a shop near Timperley's football stadium. We never went as far as pouring vinegar over the chips.... On Saturdays we went to Altrincham to do some shopping and had lunch in a Chinese restaurant. On Sunday mornings, weather permitting, all three of us went for a walk in Dunham Park, feeding the deer and drinking a glass of beer in a pub called the Swan With Two Nicks. I was breaking the law by buying a beer for my 17-year-old son as well, but these weren't the first occasions on which he drank alcohol: at the age of four I had bought a small glass of beer for him on a hot, summer day, on the terrace beside the Danube. This was not only legal but quite normal in Hungary.

I found that the atmosphere at Shell had changed. Mr Holliday, our director, had retired and his place had been taken by Bob Martin, an American. Work on fundamental research had all but stopped, and with my fresh doctoral degree I was duly transferred to process development, where amongst other duties I was put in charge of the pilot plant. I found the practical work very interesting, especially because I could immediately see the results. I had a very good team, and we were successful in doubling the output of the manufacturing plant without spending money on new equipment.

Management transferred an assistant with a history of depression to work for me. He turned out to be an excellent worker and became an asset to the team with one problem only: he was regularly ten minutes late to work, but because he often stayed on the job longer when necessary, I didn't mind. Then management transferred yet another assistant, who had just returned to work after a nervous breakdown. He too was accepted by the team and nobody complained that he did very little work to start with. Nobody except his depressive colleague, that is. The two couldn't tolerate each other, so much so that I had to separate them physically: they were put to work in different rooms, so they didn't even see one another. After this, both of them performed admirably. I consider that solving this kind of problem is part of the duties of a manager.

Bob Martin, a middle-aged scientist/manager, didn't take us to the pub for discussions as Mr Holliday had. Instead, every Wednesday morning he invited another graduate together with his boss for a discussion. The graduate was allowed to choose the subject, which didn't have to concern his own work. When my turn came I had made inquiries beforehand and found out that Bob's specialisation was organic chemical reactions. My knowledge of this subject couldn't be called excellent, so I decided to steer clear of it. His hobby was geology, and he had a nice collection of minerals, but I knew nothing about this subject either. What was left? Bob was an American, I thought, so he must be interested in money. So, I talked to him about the economics. I pointed out the huge profit margin in upgrading cheap, raw materials to high value-added products. Bob listened with great interest and supported my suggestion of expanding our manufacturing capacity.

The Last Years in England

In May of 1967 I had to visit the German chemical giant BASF together with Dr Bob Howard, my old departmental head. I had already passed my *viva* at Oxford, but hadn't yet received my diploma. Still, Bob introduced me as 'Dr Pogany', explaining the situation. For the Germans, though, this meant that I was still not a doctor and consequently they called me 'mister'.

I was lucky to have an excellent new departmental head, Don Shimmin, and I learned a lot from his management style. He was a very honest, caring, and upright person, who was against all forms of 'perks'. Once, after we had had a particularly successful episode at work, I suggested that we should organise a social evening for the staff and their partners to celebrate. As a theme, I suggested that Ted Barber, a colleague who had just returned from an assignment in South Africa, could present a selection of his pictures. To encourage the staff to participate, I suggested a photography competition of landscape pictures. I also nominated two judges and suggested a 36-exposure roll of film as the first prize, a 20-exposure roll of film as the second prize, and an honourable mention as the third prize. Don liked the idea and asked me to get on with the organisation. I did as agreed, except that I bought an extra roll of film as an afterthought.

'What's this for?' he asked me when I presented him the bill to sign.

'I thought we could reward Ted for showing his pictures as well,' I answered. But Don wouldn't have it. To him, people shouldn't expect a reward for doing something for their department. I had to keep the third roll and pay for it myself. The evening was a great success and I won third prize in the competition, but of course I didn't get anything from Don either, except a 'thank you'. I had to admit that he was right.

WHERE IS MY HOME?

Once, Don gave me a difficult job to do. 'If anyone can do it, you can,' he added.

Of course I liked a challenge, which is one of the best motivators, and I was determined to succeed. The problem was that the pilot plant worked only five days a week, and this timescale was too short to carry out any meaningful experiments. To extend the operational time, I needed the agreement of the operators, all unionised labour, known for their inflexibility. I worked out a new schedule of double-length runs, followed by double-length free time. This was accepted by all, because it allowed them to do things which were not possible in a short weekend. And so we had a ten-day uninterrupted run for our study.

My team included Allan Lancely, who was later sent to Holland to work at the laboratory in Amsterdam for a year. In his place, a Dutchman, Harry Douwes, was transferred to England. The Personnel Department wanted an easy life, and decided that the two families should simply exchange their homes for the duration of the transfer. From the point of view of the Personnel Department this was a very good idea, but it didn't work. The Dutch family, with three small children, lived in a four-room flat on the third floor of an apartment building in the middle of Amsterdam. They loved their new home, a four-bedroom, detached house in the British countryside. The English family, however, or rather Allan's wife Judy, were most unhappy with the change. From her window she couldn't see anything green, only another row of apartment houses. She had to carry her two children, one of them still a baby, in the lift every time she wanted to go out. Her hands were full and she could hardly manage to push the buttons. After about three months, they came back to England. One morning, without any warning, Allan walked into my office and reported for work. Of course he was accepted back in the lab, but they couldn't return to their now-occupied home and the Personnel Department first had to find a new furnished house to rent for the Dutch family. As it happened, this house was very near to where we lived, which resulted in a joint car-pool and a long friendship with them. In future, the Personnel Department allowed families to go and visit their new location before a transfer.

For a year I also had Bruce Klingensmith, who was in England on an exchange visit from America, working in my group. He was a good scientist with a doctoral degree in engineering and a good worker, and we also enjoyed very good social contacts. He and his charming wife, who didn't fit the stereotype of a bossy, American woman, were excellent hosts, and we drank plenty of Manhattans at their home. He had a limp and used a walking stick all the time. He was a very right-wing Republican and used to applaud the policies of President Reagan, whom he referred to simply as 'Ronald'. When I questioned him about America's enormous trade deficit, he wasn't worried: 'It's all funny money,' he used to say, lifting up his walking stick for additional emphasis. I wonder what he thinks now, after all the trouble with the banks and bad debt?

My direct boss was still Jack Mann, but our relationship had cooled somewhat. While I was in Oxford, he had published an important paper about our joint work the year before, but omitting to add my name or even acknowledge my contribution. I thought it was mean, and I still think so. Am I too vain? While Jack was in the USA for a year's assignment, and Don, our departmental head, was on a course lasting three months, he nominated me as acting departmental head. I loved it, and I also received a promotion. I tried to follow Don's good example in managing the department and was able to cope with most problems. Once, however, I was trying to push for the wrong decision, but fortunately the section head argued very forcefully against it. Finally I gave in, and just as well, because my preferred decision would have led to disaster.

With my promotion, our finances improved and Vera asked me to buy a new cooker for the kitchen. I said that as soon as we had saved up the money we would do it. Vera though was not satisfied.

'How long will it take?' she asked

'At least six months, maybe more.'

'Than we should buy it on hire purchase. Everybody does it. If we buy it from the electricity board's showroom we can pay for it on the monthly energy bill.'

I had to agree, and we bought a beautiful electric cooker, a Tricity Marquis, from which Vera got two years of pleasure. This was the only thing I ever bought on HP.

After Don returned, he sent me on a course organised by Shell for their senior staff in the chemical industries. This was a great honour and a sign not only of appreciation but also of better things to come. It lasted for four weeks, with lectures and pep talks by top managers, and we were encouraged to ask questions, to say what we didn't like, and so on. We stayed for three weeks in London, where Shell had a club, and one week in The Hague, again in a Shell club. The course ended with a three-day management game where four companies had to compete with each other. The aim was to achieve steady growth. The course made me feel important, but unduly so, because after the course I soon realised that nothing had changed. Our contact with top management remained as distant as ever.

István enrolled at Altrincham Grammar School. For years we had called him Stephen, but things changed when he became a real teenager; he had realised that sometimes it is interesting to be different. We had to call him István

The Last Years in England

again and talk to him in Hungarian only. When he went to university, we had to write to him in Hungarian. As a result, today he can converse, read, and write in Hungarian; not perfectly, but well enough.

As the time approached for István to take his O-Level exams it became more and more clear that he would not become a scientist. He had no feeling for numbers, nor was he in any way practical. One day he came to me to say that he had something very serious to discuss.

'Would you mind very much if I stopped studying chemistry?' he asked. 'My head teacher said that I could study music instead,' he added.

I didn't mind, as I knew he would never pass his exam in chemistry anyway, so I signed the form giving my consent. First he played the flute, but later we bought a clarinet for him and also paid for private tuition from a local member of the Halle Orchestra. He practiced diligently and became a member of the North of England Youth Orchestra. The greatest benefit of this was not so much the possibility of ever becoming a professional musician, but more the pleasure and relaxation he got out of it.

István had no problem meeting all the requirements for his O-Levels, except in mathematics. The rules at the time stipulated that he had to have a pass in one science subject, not necessarily maths, and he choose biology. This was a good choice, and he got the pass that enabled him to enter sixth form to study for A-Levels, which in England was necessary if he wanted to go on to university. The English sixth form, in my opinion, was then equivalent to the first year of a university course elsewhere. In the sixth form they had to study three subjects only, and he chose English language, English literature, and history. No science subject, of course. He loved to write, and his poems regularly appeared in the school magazine. He wrote prose as well, and was trying to write a novel. In the sixth form he went from strength to strength, and his teacher predicted that he would earn his living with his pen. But first we had to move to another country.

As the boss of the pilot plant, I had to supervise a day foreman and four shifts of two operators each. I had a very good relationship with all of them, mainly because I involved them in the work, the programmes, the schedules, etc. I was also very flexible, and if one was late or needed a day off we managed to cover for it. One of the operators was a Hungarian refugee, married to an English girl. He tried to develop a special relationship with me and regularly spoke to me in Hungarian at work, often in the presence of the others. I discouraged this, so I always answered him in English. Once he invited us to his home for dinner, and after a long deliberation I accepted. I must say, it was a pleasant evening, he had a charming wife who had learned how to cook an authentic Hungarian meal, and we felt that we had to reciprocate. After they visited us, however, we had no further social contact. Later, when I no longer worked at Carrington, I heard that there had been a fire in the pilot plant and that he had saved the life of one of his fellow operators. I was proud of him.

The trade union at the factory was very militant, and one day they declared that the factory was in contravention of the rules agreed with the union and withdrew their labour. Management expected this action and decided not to give in, but to fight. Non-unionised labour, including myself, were allocated jobs to operate the plant in case the operators walked out. Instructions as to what to do and how to do it were left to the shift foremen, who didn't belong to the union. It was a reversal of roles, because normally we gave the orders to him, but in the practical world of operations he was indispensable. We were given overalls, helmets, safety shoes, goggles, etc. and waited in the day foremen's room ready for action. The union started by withdrawing their labour from one of the plants, which supplied the feed to the next. The staff immediately took over the operation, and the union declared the plant 'black' and boycotted it. In such a petrochemical complex as ours, all units are connected, and as soon as another plant started to use the material from the one declared 'black' they declared this one 'black' too. One unit after the other went on strike, and we took over the operation, working in twelve-hour shifts every day for two weeks. I disagreed with the management decision not to talk to the union but instead to await their industrial action. I would have preferred it if management had continued negotiating with them, but management was eager to fight.

It all started amicably enough. On the first day of the strike, the operating shift of the pilot plant walked out as well. The pilot plant was on a different site from the main plant, and I feared that, as there was no-one to warn the incoming nightshift of the strike, they might start to work and get into trouble with their union. I returned to the pilot plant at 10pm to warn them to go home. This was much appreciated by them. The pilot plant remained shut down during the strike, since all available hands were needed on the main manufacturing plant. On the second day, after the successful operation by the staff to keep the plant working, the union convener decided not to call their action a strike, but instead a 'lock-out.' I was still joking with my own operators, who kept on coming in, mainly for gossip, that I was certainly not locking them out and that as far as I was concerned they could start working right away. But, of course, the term 'lock-out' was irrelevant. Things started to get nasty towards the end of the first week. Crowds of workers waited at the gate at each change of shift, shouting insults at us ('Scum!') and occasionally damaging our cars. So we approached the gate without our lights on and then sped out as fast as we could. It was no small miracle that nobody was run over.

Management sent notices to all striking members explaining the company's position. It was cold, logical, and written with such sophistication that ordinary workers couldn't understand it. I compared it with the simple, fiery style of the notices written by the union officials, copies of which I got from my own operators. On my advice, our management approached a PR expert to help them with writing new notices. Did it help? I don't know. I have no idea how the individual workers felt, and whether they supported their leaders from conviction or because they felt they had to. From my experience of organised labour in Hungary I was sceptical. It was also interesting to see how our own management behaved towards us. They came round quite often to show interest, asking us if we needed help, but they themselves were not working. We had to operate the works with far fewer people than normal, and it was often hard work, but I knew that there were no reserves they could call upon, so I didn't complain. They also changed their appearance, putting on scruffy clothing which blended better with our own. The food, at least, was excellent. My own shift foreman had previously been a marine engineer, and he told me: 'The first thing you noticed when there was trouble with the ship,' he said, 'was that the food got a lot better. But, of course, when the bloody ship's sinking beneath you, you work your guts out anyway!'

After two weeks the unionised workers returned to work. The company was generous to us, and we received extra pay and holidays for our efforts. Did management win? I don't think so. In a strike, as in a nuclear war, there are no

The Last Years in England

winners, only losers. The workers lost two weeks' salary for no good reason. The atmosphere at work had been spoiled, and things were no longer as harmonious as they had been before the strike. I would say that this was the start of the disintegration of that site, which is now complete.

In April of 1967 I completed ten years' service with Shell and received an emblem. I chose a tie-pin, onto which the emblem was welded. It was supposed to be made of gold, but in all likelihood only the emblem was gold, not the pin. Dan presented it to me with his congratulations, but he pointed out that I shouldn't automatically expect the next emblem, bearing a small diamond, that was given after 25 years of service. Job security had already disappeared.

In 1969, Don asked me if I would like to go to work in Shell's head office in The Hague for two years, and I immediately said 'yes'. I had already been to Holland and admired the country for its cleanliness, its efficient transport system, and of course for its flowers. I visited the Delft laboratory with two colleagues and we stayed in a hotel. In the morning I was first down for breakfast.

'How many are in your group?' asked the waiter.

'Three.'

He seated me at a table laid for three and brought coffee, a basket of bread, and three very thin slices of cheese and three equally thin slices of ham on a silver plate. I was hungry and ate them all before my colleagues arrived. The waiter was angry. 'That was meant for three people!' he exclaimed.

Later we had lunch in the canteen reserved for visitors and ate fine scallops in the shell as a starter. This raised our expectations, only to have them dashed with the next course, which was bread and tinned sardines. In the evening, though, we were lavishly treated to *rijsttafel* at an

WHERE IS MY HOME?

Indonesian restaurant. Holland is a country of gastronomic contrasts!

Because the assignment was short, Shell advised us not to sell our house but to let it furnished. Fortunately, just at this time an American engineer was transferred by Shell to England with his family and he became our tenant. On his first visit to inspect our house he asked me: 'Where do I find the restroom?'

'We haven't got one,' I replied, not realising that he meant the WC.

He came from an old family from New England and had a manner and style I had never seen before. He didn't think that the divan bed in the guest room was good enough for his daughter and insisted that I buy a new one. He also insisted on accompanying me to the shop, and kept asking the salesman: 'Is this mattress recommended for children to sleep on?' The salesman didn't really understand the question, as according to him the mattress was suitable for the queen herself to sleep on, but he remained very polite. I bought it, thinking all the while that from his American salary and expat allowance he could easily have afforded to buy it himself. Was he of Scottish descent? Towards the end of his stay he wrote me a letter saying that he was returning to the US and was 'awaiting the pleasure of the landlord', which I later learned meant that he didn't want to pay the last month's rent in full, but instead only to the exact day of his departure. I charged him half a month and deducted it from his deposit, thinking that 'possession is nine tenths of the law.'

We had the choice of either sending István to public school in England or taking him with us to Holland. He wanted to come with us, and I remember saying that if there was an opportunity for him to continue with his studies in Holland then we wanted him with us. Indeed there was

The Last Years in England

such an opportunity, and he enrolled in the British School in The Hague.

Before we went, all three of us were examined by the company's doctor and declared fit. We all received vaccinations for illnesses such as Hepatitis B, because we were going to a 'foreign' country. The fact that Holland was a much cleaner country than England didn't matter. The funny thing was, anybody transferred from Holland to England received the same treatment from his company doctor. People always feel safer amongst their own community, and going to a strange community is deemed dangerous. On that basis, I shouldn't have left Hungary, certainly not without being inoculated first!

We decided to combine our transfer, the cost of which was paid by Shell, with a European holiday. Most of our personal belongings were transported by Shell, and when the time came we wanted to pack the rest into our car but realised that there wasn't enough space for everything. We kept too much out for last-minute use, and now we had to take a few things to a friend for safe-keeping. Even so, the car was so full that not only the boot but also the back seat were full, leaving almost no space for István, who had to sit next to the vacuum cleaner. We crossed the Channel in a ferry and drove down to Switzerland for a holiday. At each stop on the way we hoped that nobody would break into the car, which by necessity remained full at night.

We very much enjoyed the scenery, which was changing from lakes to mountains. István, on the other hand, was not impressed. Every time we went up to the top of a mountain on a cable-car, he remained in our car reading Tolstoy's *War & Peace*. It's a long book, and it took him the whole holiday to finish it. Eventually, on the 15th of August, 1969, we arrived in The Hague, where we were booked in to the small Hotel Dolfijn in Scheveningen, the town's seaside resort.

WHERE IS MY HOME?

We enjoyed full board, paid by Shell, except for alcoholic drinks, which we had to pay ourselves. The manager made a suggestion: 'Bottled mineral water costs the same as a bottle of beer, so you can have beer and we'll just put "mineral water" on the bill.'

It's going to be just fine in Holland, I thought.

5
Moving to Holland.

THERE WE were, yet again, in another foreign country, but this time as expatriates not refugees. The difference was enormous. We didn't have to rely on help from the Red Cross or any other charitable organisation; our future was not uncertain; we were being looked after by our company. In fact, as an expatriate I had a higher salary than the locals. Our basic salary was adjusted to the local conditions, and on top of this we had an 'expatriate allowance.' Fewer women worked in Holland than in England, and none of the expatriate wives had jobs, so Vera became a housewife for the first time.

Our accommodation was subsidised, and we had our travel costs back home paid for once a year, while repatriation to England at the end of our stay was guaranteed. It was true that in Holland we had some extra expenses, but the net result was a surplus of cash. Alas, I would have to pay for all this luxury after my retirement, but that was far away.

After spending two weeks in the Hotel Dolfijn, we rented a furnished apartment in a pleasant area of The Hague. Our apartment had a huge living-room and three bedrooms. It was common practice in Holland to make the living-room as large as possible at the expense of the other rooms. Their kitchens were always small and often not divided off from the living-room.

The first three months of expatriate life is always pleasant, with a feeling of being on holiday at the company's expense. The 'culture shock' only kicks in after this time, when you begin to miss your home, friends, food, and, above all, your language. Culture shock makes you irritated by any little thing, which is then blown out of all proportion. It is much harder on the not-working wife than on the working husband, because she has little contact with people and stays alone all day in the flat. For Vera, the irritation was caused by the furniture in our sitting-room; the easy chairs were covered with ordinary, cheap blankets, obviously cut and sewn to fit by the owner. We bought nice, loose covers for them in England and the problem was solved.

We got out of the depression caused by the shock quickly enough by taking positive steps. We invited our neighbours, colleagues, other dog-lovers, etc. to our home. We made use of the facilities offered by the city and visited museums, concert halls, various outings, and functions organised by the office. There was even a cricket team, but I didn't join them. After about six months we started to feel comfortable in Holland, but realised that we were obviously foreigners, not even integrated yet. We again had to learn a new language, and had to start by learning a new pronunciation. The Dutch 'g' is a strange sound, coming from deep in the throat. In theory it should have been easier for a Hungarian to learn Dutch than it had been to learn English, especially if one knew some German. There are several words in Dutch similar to German and, what's more, several constructions are the same as in Hungarian. In spite of the fact that there are some English expressions in Dutch, it was easier for us to translate from Hungarian to Dutch than from English to Dutch. This was probably because both Dutch and Hungarian had been influenced by German. I said that *in theory* it should have been easier to learn Dutch, but in practice it wasn't, because our advancing age worked against us learning a new language. We again found it easier to talk to educated people, because they could more readily guess what we wanted to say, even if we didn't say it correctly.

Vera and I both attended a language laboratory run by Shell, where we had to read a Dutch text aloud while the teacher listened in to check and correct our pronunciation. We also had to learn a few common phrases and expressions. When our budget was used up we realised that we had to continue learning and called on a baby-sitting service. A plump, young girl of about eighteen, a student, duly arrived.

'Where's the baby?' she asked.

'There is no baby,' we replied. 'We just want you to talk to us in Dutch and correct us when we speak.'

We had three hours of conversation, paid her the normal rate for baby-sitting, and drove her home as a bonus. We were all satisfied and repeated this several times. Of course friends and colleagues helped us also, but several Dutch people wanted to practise their English with us in return. Educated Dutch men have a reputation of mastering several languages, but it would be a mistake to assume that they are all proficient in colloquial expressions. If for instance a colleague of mine told me that his wife was ill, on parting I would have said: 'I hope your wife will soon be better.' Not realising that this was a wish, instead of saying 'thank you' he would have replied: 'So do I.'

In general, Dutch housewives also spoke English, but less well, and they soon got tired of a long conversation. We realised that if we wanted social contacts we had to be able to speak Dutch. We invited Dutch couples for dinner and insisted on talking Dutch. When we thought that we could hold a conversation we invited two Dutch couples at the same time but this just demonstrated how little we knew. They would be talking to each other so fast that Vera and I just sat quietly, looking at each other in dismay. Another unpleasant memory I have is the first occasion when I wanted to tell a joke to a group of Dutch people. Halfway through they got fed up waiting for me to rack my brains for the right word, lost interest, and started to talk among themselves. Still, I firmly believe that you have to start talking a foreign language early on the learning process, inevitably making a fool of yourself, otherwise you never step off the curb, as it were. Eventually we mastered the language, but because we were not so young when we began learning we shall never perfect it.

Getting used to yet another different culture was not without problems either. Dutch people are very outspoken and say what's on their mind. If an Englishman wants to express his disbelief in what you've said, he says simply: 'Is that so?' meaning that he thinks you are a liar. Americans say: 'Are you kidding?' meaning much the same. Dutch people though will say directly: 'It's not true!' Our English friends found the Dutch to be rude, while Dutch people found the English politeness devious.

In spite of their apparent rudeness, Dutch people use more polite expressions than the English. They don't just say 'enjoy your meal' before eating, but also say 'enjoy the rest of your meal' after the first course. On Friday they say 'have a nice weekend,' and on a Sunday they wish you a pleasant Sunday. Complete strangers great each other when they meet out walking, in a waiting room, even in a lift. It taught us not to translate word for word, but meaning for meaning. There were plenty of *faux amis*, too. For István's birthday one year we bought a dog, a Welsh terrier. We went to the vet to ask how much food we should give her. 'One *ons*,' said the vet. We thought he meant one ounce, which is about 28 grams. It was a small dog, but still we considered 28 grams wasn't enough. Were the Dutch frugal with their pets as well? Fortunately someone explained to us that in Holland an *ons* was 100g. The price of fruit, besides, was often quoted as per *pond*, where one *pond* was exactly 500g.

After dining in the senior dining room at Carrington, it was difficult to get used to the meagre Dutch *broodmaltijd* or bread-based lunch (Dutch people, by the way, eat their sandwiches with a knife and fork). The Germans in Holland found it even more difficult, because back in Germany lunch was the main meal of the day. People in England put vinegar on their chips, while the Dutch and Belgians eat them with mayonnaise. Dutch coffee is stronger than English, and in the canteen English people used to dilute their coffee with hot water. Instead of hot milk, a little condensed milk is used, so as not to cool the coffee down. We, of course, liked the stronger coffee, which was still weaker than the Hungarian. But if I had to choose one Dutch national dish, it would not be the cheese, but the raw herring. People can't wait for the new catch, which arrives in the shops in June, and they eat it with chopped onion and pickled gherkin. I must say I like it too, together with the national drink of buttermilk, *karnemelk*.

Almost every man in Holland drinks one or two glasses of *genever*, or 'Dutch gin', before dinner. Ladies prefer something sweeter, like a port or a white wine. But dinner invitations in Holland were less frequent than they were in England. We had to remember all these customs and made sure to use the right one according to the nationality of our guest at the time. We did offer them Hungarian *pálinka* as well, but only as an alternative to *genever*. They politely tried it, then invariably returned to their *genever*.

Some of my English colleagues didn't like the cuts of meat in the shops. They missed the English 'joint', and found a butcher who was prepared to sell half a pig, cut to the customer's requirements. Once we also bought half a pig and put it into the deep-freeze, but we found that we were eating more meat than was good for us and didn't repeat the order.

The form of a dinner party was also different in Holland. When the visitors arrived, the men shook hands while there was a compulsory exchange of three (!) kisses on the cheek between the opposite sexes. An after-dinner invitation always started with two cups of coffee with half an hour's interval. This was supposed to be in place of the after-dinner coffee which the guests would have drunk at home. Only after that were alcoholic drinks offered, usually two but occasionally three glasses of wine, again with half an hour's interval. Some form of sweet was offered with the coffee, and savoury snacks with the alcoholic drinks. Dutch people would never drink alcohol without having some snacks to go with it. There are fewer dinner invitations than in England, as Dutch housewives don't like to spend much time in the kitchen.

It's common knowledge that you can't always translate jokes into another language, and it took us a long time to understand, never mind to appreciate, Dutch jokes, which are often more crude than the subtle English ones. We had already forgotten that most Hungarian jokes were very similar to Dutch ones. Dutch comedians would draw applause simply by pulling funny faces. One of the most popular one was André van Duin, who always liked to play the idiot by continuously pulling his lips to one side. But after we managed to learn more Dutch, we appreciated the political jokes of the late Wim Kan and other entertainers like that great charmer, the late Toon Hermans.

Like everybody else, Dutch people think that their country and their language is the most beautiful in the world. One day, someone asked me a difficult question: 'What do you miss in Holland?' I had to think hard to say something which could not possibly offend her, and said: 'I miss the mountains.' I thought I was on safe ground, as the highest point in Holland is just 300 meters, and even this is shared by three countries. But she was not satisfied.

'Don't you think that the cloud formations in the sky

above the polders are just as beautiful?' Only after I had said that I preferred the Alps did I realise that I had upset her.

Apart from their windmills, tulips, and wooden clogs, Dutch people also have a reputation for being frugal. The people of The Hague are supposed to be even more frugal than the rest of the country, but I found no evidence for this. Endless jokes are made by Belgians about Dutch frugality, and in return there are just as many jokes in Holland about the supposedly simple-minded Belgians. I found it a paradox, that while most Dutch people were indeed careful with their money, at the same time Holland gave more to charity per capita than any other nation. It took me some time to understand the love of the Dutch for the *Poldermodel*, a desire for consensus-based policy-making wherever possible, or for an acceptable compromise if necessary. Prostitution, soft drugs, and euthanasia, for example, were all illegal, but tolerated. This way, both conservatives and progressives had their way. Everybody had a right to higher education, so university entry was based not on merit but on the luck of the draw

We found life more competitive than in England. Dutch people on the whole liked order, but there were no queues, and people just pushed their way through the crowd. We had season tickets to concerts, and in the interval we too wanted a cup of coffee. Our son would go to the bar, but was the last person to be served. With his English upbringing he was not pushy and would let everyone go in front of him. Driving was also more competitive: a flash of the headlights would not give you the right of way, but should be taken as warning or disapproval.

Because my assignment was for a period of just two years, we put less effort into integration than we would have done otherwise. Most of our friends were also expatriates, and

WHERE IS MY HOME?

we talked mainly English. Strangely, I found that we were less readily accepted by those members of the expatriate British community who didn't know us than had been the case in England. They immediately realised from our pronunciation that we were from another country. Living abroad, they were suspicious of everyone and everything foreign, and this included us. This was disturbing, because we thought that we had integrated well into English society but now realised that we remained to these expats just more 'bloody foreigners'.

The Hague had a very international community. It had several foreign-language schools, and clubs like the Commonwealth Club and the British Women's Club, and soon after we arrived we were approached to join them, which we did. The language was English not only in the clubs but also at work, almost everywhere in the city. I asked one of my English colleagues, who had already spent several years in The Hague, how long it had taken to learn Dutch. 'Me?' he answered. 'I make a point of learning one new word every year.'

We had several friends amongst the expatriate community, mainly English, and we could joke about Dutch bureaucracy, the food, and the lack of queuing. A colleague of mine, Richard, one day left the office at lunch time and I asked him where he was going. 'To the post office,' he said, 'to get a TV licence.'

'Have you filled in all the forms?' I enquired rather mischievously. 'Sure,' he said. 'I also have three pictures of the TV set with me.' Richard had brought not only his wife but also her mother with him to Holland. The old lady was getting on for eighty, but still had to have a bottle of Guinness every day, imported from England.

Moving to Holland

On my birth certificate my given names are Sándor György. Sándor was the name of my grandfather, but I was always called Gyuri, which is short for György. When we arrived in England I realised that no-one could pronounce my Hungarian names, so I converted my names to George Alexander, and used the George only. I didn't have my birth certificate with me, but in England this was no problem, and I now have these names on my naturalisation document and also on my British passport. By the time we arrived in Holland I had my birth certificate with me, and foolishly presented it at the town hall for permission to be resident. I told the clerk that I was using the names George Alexander, but he insisted on writing down the original name on my birth certificate, with accents and all. I became George Alexander at work, at the bank, and at the tax office, but Sándor György on my driving licence, and this still gives me endless trouble when I try to identify myself with it.

We retained our British nationality and were considered foreigners in Holland by the authorities. We had to renew our residence permit regularly, even after the UK and Holland were both members of the European Union. The fact that nobody ever asked for it was unimportant. Eventually we got permission to reside permanently and received a card, resembling a credit card but with a photo, to prove our identity. Nevertheless, this card still has an expiry date! Because we retained our British nationality, we have no voting rights in Holland. We got used to these small inconveniences, and saw no reason to change our nationality yet again.

A great attraction for us was the proximity of the sea. Having lived for almost thirty years in a landlocked country, I loved the endless water, the breeze, and the smell of salt in the air. On weekends we used to walk our dog on the beach, and in the summer on the dunes, which were covered with green grass. In several occasions we braved the cold water and went swimming either in Scheveningen or in the nearby Wassenaarse Slag. Scheveningen was very commercial, with lots of tents serving snacks and refreshments right on the beach. At first I thought I had to use their facilities if I wanted to swim, because the tents were erected so close to each other, like stalls at a market. On the shore there were hotels and restaurants for all tastes and budgets. Wassenaarse Slag was more unspoiled, and we preferred it to the busy and commercial Scheveningen. Unfortunately we were not the only ones, and if we didn't start really early we found ourselves in a long queue with hardly any place to park. Still it was worth it. It's funny how looking at the sea, even when it's rough, soothes the nerves.

Recognising that they are in the minority, some expatriates can develop a feeling of inferiority, and a few can react with aggression. Of course there are differences in language, culture, and customs between different countries, but these needn't be a source of irritation, but of enjoyment. We found that the secret of happiness was to acknowledge these differences but not to put value on them by calling one better than the other. We were different, but we were both OK. For integration it is not necessary to change one's identity. The time I spent in Oxford, where I met many people from different cultures, was good training.

My boss invited us on one occasion for a typical Dutch meal of *erwtensoep*, a thick pea soup that traditionally came with black bread and cooked pig's trotter. We noticed how his home, a typical Dutch one, was differently furnished from those in England. There was no wall-to-wall carpeting, and the parquet floor was covered by a few Persian rugs instead. The walls were painted light yellow and were covered with paintings and an antique clock, which in turn was covered

Moving to Holland

with an embroidered cloth. There were several antique vases on the top of an antique wardrobe. As he told me: 'I like to look at beautiful things.' To this remark my East-European nature compelled me to add: 'So that's why you always like to sit opposite your wife!' Even for such a simple meal, the dinner table was beautifully laid and lots of candles were burning in the room. The living-room walls were covered with huge bookshelves full of books. The curtains were not drawn, and anyone walking on the street could see inside.

'We have nothing to hide,' he said, when he saw my surprise. When we invited them back for our Transylvanian goulash, he managed to knock over his glass of red wine twice during the meal. Obviously he was a theoretician with no laboratory experience. This boss had a PhD in engineering, but I always considered him an accountant, since he used to check my calculations even when they had been made by a computer. After his retirement he wrote a book comparing the management styles of Shell and the Vatican. I could have added to this comparison the management style of the communist countries. Of course, in Shell or in the Vatican there was no gulag, and people were not shot or imprisoned, but strong hierarchical structures have many similarities.

The home of another colleague of mine was quite different. They had employed an interior designer to design their living-room, and the result had been an ugly, dark green colour which covered everything—the walls, the doors, even the grand piano. They liked it and were proud of it, but I think it was the result of a midlife crisis.

Family ties were very strong in Holland. The birthday of any member of the family was an important date and couldn't be missed. Not only close relatives, but also uncles, aunts, nephews, girlfriends, etc. all had to come to visit the birthday boy or girl and congratulate not only him or her but all those present besides. A special family get-together was the celebration of the arrival of Saint Nicholas from Spain, who looked remarkably like Father Christmas. Every member of the family prepared a gift for all the rest, accompanied by a poem, supposedly written by Saint Nicholas himself, which, in a humorous way, poked fun at the recipient. It was a great honour when my colleague Harry and his wife Thea invited us to their family celebration. We felt that we had been fully accepted as their friends. Is this all it took to feel integrated into Dutch society?

There were some 3,000 people working in the head offices of Shell in The Hague, and the offices occupied almost a whole street. As in Shell Carrington, on my first day in the office I went for a walk during the lunch break with a Dutch colleague. I noticed a signboard at the entrance to the adjacent park, listing a number of things which were forbidden, like walking on the grass, having a dog without a leash, and so forth. I commented that I found it strange that so many things were forbidden, to which my Dutch colleague replied: 'If the sign says simply "*verboden*", we take no notice. To take it seriously it has to say "*streng verboden*".'

This was an exciting time for Shell, as the company was vastly expanding its activities in the production of chemicals. For the first time, one of the top seven managing directors had the chemical business added to his portfolio of duties. His office was on the same floor as mine, and I used to meet him in the gents'. At the Christmas party he made a speech, predicting that the time was approaching when Shell's chemical business would exceed that of its oil business. How wrong he was!

The Central Office in London was responsible for marketing and finance, while the Hague Central Office looked after manufacturing and technology. My duties were to look after the polystyrene business, with which I had been intimately connected for years. Business was booming, and we were busy expanding capacity. We also needed new pilot plant facilities and went to England to investigate whether we could hire a pilot plant there. One of the potential sites we looked at was in Wales, near to a former coal mine. They indeed had spare reactor capacity, and we asked if they could treat the waste products safely. 'Sure,' they said with a big smile. 'We can just pour it down into the disused mine shaft. Nobody will ever find it.' We didn't recommend them.

Ron L. became my departmental head in The Hague. Before making any decision about an investment, he asked for lots of financial evaluations considering all kinds of options, such as where to invest and how big the plant should be. We had just started using computers and had to feed our assumptions into the machine by punching a number of cards, and the process was rather tedious and time-consuming, but still he always asked for more. Eventually, often fate made the decision for him, as we would miss the boat because of his delays. He also knew how to manipulate the calculations to get the result he wanted. I'm not saying that this was wrong, only that in spite of the scientific approach to decision-making that gave an impression of objectivity, the assumptions had determined the outcome and the decision was always subjective.

There was a lively Hungarian community in the Hague, but because we had come via England we didn't become active members. János U., a mechanical engineer, had managed to defect from Hungary in 1971 and had joined Shell. Because of his advanced age he would have been eligible for a small pension only, so Shell granted him another ten years of service and paid the pension fund the missing contribution.

WHERE IS MY HOME?

He was an excellent engineer, but suffered from bouts of depression.

Another Hungarian, Albert M., working for Shell in Amsterdam, had been my colleague in Budapest at Vegyterv. He too suffered from depression, and one evening at 11pm he reported to work at the laboratory. The porter had to call his boss, who managed to persuade him to go home. Albert had a Hungarian wife and two boys, but he left them and rented a small apartment, claiming that he needed to be alone to get to know himself. I think he was simply promiscuous. Once I met his new mistress and found her ugly.

'Your wife's much more beautiful than this woman,' I told him afterwards.

'Why does a woman have to be beautiful?' he retorted. Why indeed? Some men want to look at beautiful women, others might want to show her off. How can you explain physical attraction?

On another occasion Albert lit a large number of candles in his apartment and the neighbours called the fire brigade. Eventually he was taken to an institution and later died. We were friends with his wife and kept in contact after his death. We tried to find a match for her, and once set her up with a single man we had met at one of our holidays. Unfortunately, instead of getting to know him she flirted with me and this made Vera jealous and stopped any further contact with her. Many years later I was lying in hospital, and one of the nurses told me that she had a Hungarian boyfriend. She named him, and I recognised him as one of the sons of my late friend Albert, now a doctor. It's a small world, and Holland is even smaller.

While in the work camp, during the war, I never saw anyone depressed, even though we certainly had more reason for it. Do poor people suffer from depression just as

Moving to Holland

much? Is it connected to race or religion? Fortunately none of our family has had a problem with it.

We became rather friendly with a Hungarian couple Susan and Bandi, who in 1956 had emigrated to Belgium and had later come to Holland. We visited them just as they were busy hanging up some pictures.

'Not there!' shouted Susan at her husband. 'Further to the left! I've told you before, haven't I, that it has to hang exactly halfway between the chimney and the Vermeer! Can't you see it's too far to the right? And why did you have to make such a big hole? Did you put the nail in headfirst? Now you've spoiled the wallpaper! This is a man's job, but you're too clumsy even for something as simple as putting a picture on the wall!'

'Yes, my little rabbit,' answered Bandi, standing uncomfortably on a chair. 'I'm sorry, I'll try it again.'

'Don't call me "little rabbit"!' shouted his wife, almost in a rage. 'Every time you make a mess of something, you call me "little rabbit"!'

'But I *always* call you "little rabbit"!' he protested.

'That's because you're *always* messing things up! Why can't you be as handy as other men? I tell you why, because you don't try hard enough. You're too lazy, that's your trouble. Look at David! He decorated their whole house and even put up the wainscot in their hall. *And* he's a successful, wealthy lawyer!' Susan went on. 'And what are you? You're an average, run-of-the mill civil servant without any hope of promotion. You certainly can't put a nail in the wall at the right place! Tell me what you're good at besides eating and watching television?'

Bandi had to think a little. 'I can play the piano,' he said finally, with a light in his eyes. He even risked a smile as he added: 'David can't...,' but he couldn't finish the sentence, because the doorbell rang.

'My God, they're here already! I should've known! David isn't like you, he's always punctual!' And with those words Susan took off her apron, licked her fingers, smoothed her long, black, false eyelashes and ran to the door. She was a small woman, almost half the size of her husband, with a slender figure. She dyed her long hair platinum blond and always carefully matched the colour of her dress with the colour of her lipstick and nail varnish. She used so much perfume that one could smell it throughout the house. Bandi was a total contrast to his wife and didn't possess her endless energy and activity. He had studied music in Hungary, but hadn't been good enough to earn his living as a professional musician and so had studied chemistry and earned a diploma. Bandi accepted life as it came, Susan included, to whom he gave various pet names. He was overweight, quiet, always polite, pleasant company, and took his wife's bossiness in his stride with no indication that it irritated him. They had been married for twenty-four years and had no children. After the Hungarian revolution they had lived in Brussels, where Susan had got hooked on the French lifestyle. From there onwards everything she did, bought, and cooked was French. Now that they had moved on a temporary assignment to the Hague it was not so easy to continue this, but Susan regularly went back to Brussels to do her shopping there. She liked to show off to their new Dutch friends with her French cuisine. Amongst their new friends, apart from us, David and Thea were the most important. They were not only rich and influential; they also had good taste, had an international outlook and appreciated good food. They had an extended circle of prestigious friends and Susan had hoped that she too would be accepted by them.

Moving to Holland

Bandi climbed down from the chair and placed the reproduction Rembrandt against the wall under the spot where it should have been hung. He just had time to put on his jacket when David and Thea entered the room carrying the customary bunch of flowers. They were roses, twelve beautiful stems, rolled up in paper proudly exhibiting the name of the most expensive flower shop in The Hague.

Susan excelled again in her *paté de chef de maison*, which she made from chicken liver. She never admitted this to anyone, always claiming that it was made from calf's liver. The main course was *osso bucco provincial*. It was the generous amount of garlic that made the difference between hers and the traditional Italian dish. As is a must in Belgium, it was served with chips, and in turn the chips had to be consumed by dipping them in mayonnaise. Dinner ended with her favourite sweet, 'orange surprise' served in the scooped-out skins of fresh oranges. After coffee and brandy we said goodbye, went home, and later reconstructed the rest of the evening from Bandi's recollections.

Susan had decided to take the dog out for a walk, and David had thought it was only polite to accompany her, while Thea had volunteered to clear the table. She was a typical Dutch housewife, dressed simply, used no make-up, and wore her long, blond hair on the top of her head. She was neither beautiful nor ugly, but had a pleasant, direct nature, always smiling at whomever she was talking with. Bandi, who had nothing better to do, sat down at the piano and started to play his favourite melodies, a mixture of Hungarian Gypsy music and a few popular French *chansons*. He was happily singing along, forgetting all about the pictures, Susan, and their guests. Suddenly he noticed the silence, stopped playing, and turned round. Thea was standing right behind him, and she now put her hand on his shoulder in encouragement.

WHERE IS MY HOME?

'I didn't mean to startle you,' she said. 'Please continue!' Then she added in a soft, flattering tone: 'You Hungarians, you're so romantic and have so much feeling. Did anyone tell you that you play beautifully? Where does it all come from? How can you hide it? What a strange man you are, Bandi! Inside that big, strong body of yours is a sensitive child.'

Bandi was deeply touched by this remark; Susan never talked to him like that.

'Do you really think I'm more romantic than David?' he asked finally, obviously fishing for compliments.

'*Especially* David. Not only can't he play an instrument, he has no appreciation of any form of art. But you're different, and I could go on listening to you forever.'

Bandi hadn't previously looked at Thea as anything but a friend with whom he occasionally played a game of bridge. But now he changed the tune and started playing a slow melody: *'For me, there is only one girl in this whole world....'* He was singing in Hungarian, but Thea could feel its meaning from the tone and from the look in his eyes.

'...And there is nothing I'd like more, than to play for you,' he added with a hitherto unseen enthusiasm. Thea had smiled as she leant forward and kissed him lightly. She didn't have to lean too much, since Bandi, even when sitting, was so tall. She had stayed behind him, now with both hands around his neck while he continued to strike the keyboard with great enthusiasm. The tunes didn't matter anymore; he could have played a funeral march, for all they cared.

It was a rainy, Friday evening some month or so later, when, on leaving my office, I noticed Bandi sitting in his small Renault in front of the building. To be truthful, I hardly recognised him, he'd lost so much weight.

'What are you doing here?' I asked him.

'Waiting for you,' was his obvious answer. 'I was in the

area and thought I'd give you a lift home.' But at the roundabout he took the wrong turn and headed toward the city. He stopped in front of a small coffee bar and invited me in.

'What will Susan say when you don't turn up for dinner on time?' I asked. 'You know she doesn't like her food spoiled.'

'I don't eat her food anymore, I've gone on a diet.'

'Is that why you lost so much weight?'

'So you have noticed?' smiled Bandi, and pulled his loosely hanging jacket away from his stomach to show how much was missing. 'Yes, I like it better this way.'

'And what does Susan say about this?' I insisted, bringing her back into the conversation. Bandi stopped smiling.

'She's the one I want to talk to you about.' He ordered two glasses of beer and explained what had happened between him and Thea after we had left the dinner party, and then he continued: 'I can't stand Susan anymore. You know that she's no feelings in her, certainly not for me, nor for anything else, I guess, except for a few grandiose ideas. Tell me, why does she need that huge Citroen? We can hardly afford it. And her taste! Have you seen that new wallpaper in our living-room? The one with the purple peacocks? Did you know it was hand-painted, and that she ordered it especially from Paris? And that's not enough! She has to hang reproductions of old Dutch masters on the same wall! Sober Rembrandts and Vermeers in thick, brown frames, hung in between those birds. You know I'm an artist? It hurts me!' This was the first time I'd heard him call himself an artist. But he hadn't finished yet. 'You should see our bedroom! That's where she *really* got going. We've a four-poster bed with brass knobs on each corner. The chair is reproduction Louis XV. The chandelier's so heavy, one of these days it'll fall down and kill us both! But that's nothing compared to what I have to suffer because of her bossiness. I can't do or say *anything*. You know what she did the last time we ate in a restaurant? *She* actually selected and ordered the wine. I ask you! Is that normal? When the waiter opened the bottle, he hesitated, than offered it to *her* to try. I was hoping the floor would open up under my chair, I was so ashamed….'

'But you've lived together for so long,' I said with some sympathy. 'It didn't all change suddenly.'

'You're right,' he agreed, emptying half of his beer in one large gulp. 'But I tell you what *has* changed suddenly—I've fallen in love with another woman.'

'You're joking!'

'No, it's true.'

'Who did you fall in love with?' I somehow couldn't visualise anyone who could have shaken up Bandi so drastically.

'With Thea,' he answered after some hesitation. 'David's wife,' he added, to make certain I understood. 'I've asked her to marry me.'

'You asked her to *what*?' I could sympathise with him in trying to leave Susan, but found it difficult to understand how, if he was so unhappy with his first wife, he could get involved with another woman so seriously and so quickly? Talk about jumping out of the frying pan into the fire. 'And what about Thea? What did she say to your proposal?'

'She loves me too….'

'That's not what I asked,' I interrupted. 'Did she say yes? Did she agree to leave David and marry you?'

'Not yet,' he admitted after a long pause and a deep sigh. He ordered two more beers with *genever* chasers. 'She wanted to think it over but promised to give me her decision tomorrow. I know she'll say yes, I can feel it, she's so romantic, full of feelings. Do you know, when we're playing bridge, when she bids one heart, she points to her heart at the same time? I could cry just to remember it.'

Moving to Holland

'It could be a secret signal to her partner to say that her suit's long or her hand's extra strong,' I ventured to comment, none too romantically, but Bandi was not pleased. Then he added as an afterthought:

'She has to say yes!'

'OK, let's suppose she *will* say yes. Then what will you do? Susan will stay in your house and you'll have to pay her alimony. At the same time, Thea will have to move out of their house and won't receive a cent from her husband. She's got used to the good life, you know.'

'Oh, you don't know her!' said Bandi. 'She's a delicate, refined person, who appreciates art. Material wealth doesn't interest her. I told her I'll bring the guest bed, a table, and two chairs with me, and of course the piano. That's all we'll need. We've discussed all this already.'

'Don't you think it's all happening much too quickly? Have you thought it through? You know how they say the grass is always greener on the other side of the fence? It might be the same with women. Meeting someone now and again isn't the same as living with them day after day. I knew someone in England who married her ideal lover, but she was so unhappy with him as a husband. Shouldn't you wait?' But Bandi was in no mood to change either speed or direction. He'd made his mind up, and that was that. 'And have you told Susan?' I asked. Bandi only answered after a long pause, first drinking some more beer, then sipping at his *genever*.

'No, not yet. I haven't the courage.' Then, after a little while, he added sheepishly: 'I thought, perhaps, you might do it for me. Surely that's what friends are for. I'll phone you when I know for certain.'

Next evening Vera and I played bridge at our club, came home late, and went straight to bed. The telephone woke us at 5am. It was Susan.

WHERE IS MY HOME?

'Is Bandi with you?' she asked, without apologising for calling at such an unearthly hour.

'No, should he be?' There was silence, than a sobbing voice.

'I don't know. I don't know anything anymore.' She found it difficult to continue. 'He came home last night at six as usual, but didn't say a word, didn't touch his meal, just started drinking and hitting the piano. Then he got into his car and disappeared without even saying goodbye. I haven't heard from him since. You're his best friend; I thought he might be with you.' She didn't wait for my reply, just hung up.

I couldn't get back to sleep after that, so I got up, squeezed an orange, and made myself a cup of coffee and some toast. After glancing through the morning paper I went over to Susan's. I rang the bell, but there was no answer. I knew she was at home, because her Citroen was parked on the drive. I walked round the side of the house and found the kitchen door open. The sound of Edith Piaf's famous *Non, Je Ne Regrette Rien* was coming from the living room at full volume. Instead of Susan's exquisite perfume, the whole house smelt of cigarette smoke. Entering the room, I immediately noticed that the walls were empty, that all the reproductions had been taken down. Those purple peacocks were looking at me more sadly than ever. Susan was sitting in front of the record player, an over-full ashtray in her lap. She didn't notice me at all, so busy was she trying to recover the last drops from a bottle of brandy.

'I took them down for him,' she said finally, after my greeting, obviously referring to the pictures. 'I knew he didn't like them. I even told him we could redecorate the room if he wanted to. We could have robins instead of peacocks. But he never said a word. Where is he George? What happened to him? Did he have an accident, or is he with another woman?' Poor Susan, I had never seen her before without any make-up. She was wrapped up in a tatty dressing gown, and her hair was full of rollers. I stayed a while, comforting her, saying that Bandi was big enough to look after himself, and that had there been an accident she would have heard about it by now. I didn't know what else to do, as Bandi hadn't contacted me. Should I tell her, or shouldn't I?

'Have you noticed anything about him lately?' I asked.

'Yes, I have. When he refused to eat his plum dumpling I knew that something must've happened. It was always his favourite,' she said. 'He'd bought a diet book and started to count the calories.'

'Was there anything else?' I urged, hoping that my job might get easier. She thought carefully before answering.

'Not really, not until last night.' Then suddenly she added: 'Except for one thing, he always wanted to invite David and Thea for a whole weekend. I ask you! You know how small this flat is?' Then her voice started to tremble: 'You don't mean that he and Thea…?' Without waiting for my answer she started to cry, emptied her glass, lit another cigarette, and put Edith Piaf on again at full volume. 'Thea, of *course* Thea, I might have known. I never liked her! She's like a spoiled child! She's got everything in life and still she's not satisfied! She wants *everything!* Now she's robbed me of the only precious thing I had, the only man I've ever loved! Oh, you'll never understand how much he means to me. He's such a wonderful man, cheerful, strong, good-looking, reliable, always there when I needed him.' She blew her nose and continued in a whine: 'I'm lost without him, completely lost….'

I didn't know what to say. Should I suggest she say all this directly to her husband? I had no authority to confirm the story about Thea, but I couldn't deny it either. 'There must be some very simple explanation,' I said finally, 'which you'll hear from Bandi soon enough.' Somehow I couldn't imagine Thea saying 'yes' to him. I expected her to be more sensible than that. In the end, Susan fell asleep in one of the Louis XV chairs. I walked out, closed the door, and went home.

Bandi was sitting on our porch, waiting for me. He had no jacket, no tie, and no shoes on his large feet. There was a big, wet patch on his white shirt, and his trousers were fastened with a rolled-up plastic bag on which the name of a supermarket was legible.

'I saw your car was out and I didn't want to bother Vera, so I waited for you. Can I use your bathroom?' he asked without explanation. I think he didn't want to meet Vera because he was so ashamed of himself. But after a bath, and a sumptuous breakfast prepared by Vera, he started talking.

'Would you believe it? Thea turned me down. The bitch wouldn't part with that comfortable lifestyle of hers. She's just like Susan, you know, no difference at all. Her only concern was that I shouldn't say a word to her husband. What does she think I am?'

'Well, that much I expected,' I said with some satisfaction. 'I'm a better judge of character than you are.'

'What could I do?' continued Bandi without reflecting on my comment. 'You know I'm an artist, and when an artist wants to bury his sorrows he must practise his art. While I was playing my piano, it suddenly became crystal clear to me that I didn't belong to anyone and anywhere; my life had lost its meaning, so I had to end it. I decided to commit suicide.'

'You decided *what?!*'

'When I got into my car I'd already decided to drive it straight into something, but somehow I couldn't find anything to smash into until I'd already driven to Amsterdam. I thought, I might as well have a drink first, so I went to a bar and found myself staying there until closing time.'

'That must have been around midnight, so what have you been doing since? And what happened to your clothes?'

'I met these three students. At least, they *said* they were students, but for the life of me I can't remember what they studied. They said they knew a place that stayed open all night. I still had plenty of money on me….'

'And the fool you are, you went with them.'

'Sure I did, why shouldn't I? It was going to be my last evening, remember? But it was a rough place.'

'I can imagine.'

'Of course, I was paying.'

'Of course!'

'I don't know how it happened, but when it came to paying the bill I couldn't find my wallet. It'd disappeared.'

'Of course.'

'You don't think *they* took it? They were such nice people! They even introduced me to a couple of their girlfriends.'

'That was nice of them!'

'Yes it was, especially the one with the dark hair, Carmen. She was very friendly. When I couldn't pay the bill, they started searching through my pockets and took anything they could find. They said they had to, otherwise the owner would've called the police. I couldn't commit suicide in jail, could I?'

'Well, not without your belt and shoelaces,' I agreed. 'But what happened to your car? Did your nice friends take that too?'

'You see, this is the bit I don't remember. I had no idea where I'd left my car. But when I left the pub, I must've turned the right way, because suddenly there it was. And you know what? The door was open and the key was in the ignition. How did it get there?'

'But where's your car now?' I asked, without feeling obliged to answer his question. 'How did you get here without it?'

'Don't hurry me, I'm coming to that. But I'm tired, and all this is giving me a headache,' said Bandi, and wiped his forehead with his handkerchief. 'I was driving out of the city, still thinking of suicide, and suddenly I noticed a canal. I took a deep breath and drove straight into it.'

'Jesus!' I cried. 'And how did you get out of it?'

'I read somewhere, that people just about to die see their whole life flash before their eyes in a single minute. I remembered my childhood, then my schooldays, but when I got to my marriage I began to suspect that more than a minute had gone past. It turned out to be one of those shallow irrigation canals the local farmers use. I stepped out of the car into ankle-deep water....'

'And instead of meeting St Peter, I suppose you were greeted by the police?'

'How do you know?'

'Just intuition,' I said modestly, but Bandi was not amused.

'I failed!' he cried. 'Susan's right, I'm hopeless! I couldn't even kill myself properly!'

For the next week we were marriage-guidance counsellors to the two of them. Vera talked to Susan, slowly persuading her to forgive Bandi, while in a separate room I was all the while talking to Bandi, suggesting he accept Susan as she was. It worked, and they resumed their lives together again.

Six months later it was their silver wedding anniversary, and we were invited. Everybody was there, with the notable exception of David and Thea. Susan again demonstrated her talent by preparing an exquisite cold buffet with a selection of shrimps, smoked salmon, and eel, together with Hungarian salami. There was chilled Riesling to go with the fish, and Hungarian *bikavér*—'bull's blood' wine—to accompany the salami. The room was decorated with coloured balloons and paper chains. The Dutch masters were hanging in their usual places, surrounded by the purple peacocks.

'Bandi!' shouted Susan as she put two logs on the big, open fire. 'There's no more wood. Will you be a good boy and bring some from the garage? That's a man's job, isn't it?'

Bandi stood stock still, his eyes seeking out mine. They were red, and for a moment I thought he would throw the half-full *genever* bottle he was holding at his wife. But it lasted only a moment, and then his eyes became expressionless. He lifted up those big shoulders of his and then let them drop again.

'Yes, my little rabbit,' he said. 'Of course.' And he picked up the empty log-tray and walked out of the room.

We continued our friendship, and a couple of times went on holiday together. On one of these occasions the weather turned so bad that we decided to stay in the hotel all day, and this was a good time to play bridge. Later Bandi got a transfer to Munich and Susan asked us to come to their farewell party. We had another engagement on that day, and anyway we don't like big parties, the kind when the host and hostess are too busy to talk to you. We said goodbye, and told them we weren't able to come to the party. Susan didn't take this lightly. I suppose she wanted to show off how many friends they had.

'If you're not coming, we'll never see each other again,' she warned us. We didn't believe her, but she kept her word.

WHERE IS MY HOME?

István attended the English school in Scheveningen, with the children of British expatriates—diplomats, business executives, and the like—who were often sent to different countries. They also lived very busy lives, and this was reflected by the way they brought up their children. Some of them had too much freedom and too much pocket money, and the school became a place to try out soft drugs like marijuana. István was following a proper English syllabus for his A-Levels, which he passed with flying colours. His headmaster was impressed with his ability to write in English, and predicted that one day he would earn his living as a writer. Indeed, he has written several books and numerous articles in learned journals. For a long time he didn't know what he wanted to do, but when he was chosen to represent England in a mock UN meeting organised between all the international schools in The Hague, he made his decision and studied international public law. After his A-Levels he went to the University of Edinburgh. It is one of the ironies of life that, while I came to England partly to have my son educated in Oxford, I myself went there but my son wouldn't have even considered it.

In his first letter home from Edinburgh he wrote that his fellow students were enthusiastic about the freedom they enjoyed, being away from home for the first time. István said to them that he had already had such freedom, but that he was missing his mother's cooking. I think it was the nicest compliment I ever got from him. One day, we found out that he was occasionally buying a bottle of cider with his friends to drink in a park somewhere.

'Why in the park?' we asked him. 'Why not at home?' To his great surprise we allowed him to ask his friends back home, and we prepared some food to go with the cider—which they still had to buy themselves.

Moving to Holland

Following in his father's footstep, at the age of nineteen István found Ruth, a nice student at the same university, and they decided to move in together. Ruth, who later became his wife, had no financial help from her parents and only a government scholarship, so we increased the support we were giving István. Still, they had to live very modestly in an apartment of just one room and a kitchen, without even a bathroom. They had to wash themselves using the hot water from a kitchen boiler, and for a bath they used a large, plastic dustbin. On one of István's visits to us we bought for them a small, plastic bathtub, which he took with him on the boat and the train all the way back to Edinburgh.

A couple of years later they decided to get married, and we travelled to London to be there on the day. As a wedding present we bought a crate of champagne for the reception. Ruth's parents were very religious and also teetotallers, but István had got used to drinking in Scotland. On their wedding day he went to the station with Ruth's sixteen-year-old brother to collect his best man, who was coming from Edinburgh. They had some time on their hands, so the three of them first visited a pub before coming to the church. We and Ruth's parents were sitting in the first row, with the brother and the other relatives sitting further back. During the sermon we heard a big thump and, looking round, I saw the brother lying on the floor. I went to help him and was struck by the smell of whisky. On my return to my seat I had to tell his teetotal parents that there was nothing wrong with him, that he was only drunk.

Sadly, Ruth was suffering from a rare lung disease, and she died at the age of 52 without having children.

WHERE IS MY HOME?

István and Ruth

6

Delft

WHILE I liked my work, it became clear that I was not a political animal, and not suited for permanent head office work. When my two-year assignment was nearing its end I began considering my future. There were clear signs that Shell were about to close the research laboratory in England where I used to work, and I thought it would be better if I stayed in Holland. This was at least possible, since there was a vacancy in the plastics research laboratory at Delft (the 'Koninklijke Shell Plastics Laboratorium Delft', or KSPLD), and my assignment was extended by another two years.

The laboratory at Delft was doing applied research, developing new applications for the polymers the Shell factories produced as well as providing technical services for our customers. There were about 350 people employed, which meant that almost everybody knew everybody else. The director, Dr Goppel, was rather authoritarian but was not only respected, but almost revered by everybody. Contact between people was informal and rather friendly. There was a feeling of belonging to a large family.

I had visited the laboratory while I was still working in England, but never thought that one day I would be working there. I was put in charge of the analytical department, whose boss has just retired. In spite of the fact that this position had a lower job group rating, I accepted it; they promised that my salary would not be reduced. It was not, but only by accident did I later find out that I had in fact been demoted. About ten people worked in my department, and for the first time I was in charge of a group of Dutch workers.

If there was a subject at my university course which I had disliked, it was analytical chemistry. And here I was, the boss of the analytical department. I had to supervise a team of ten assistants, all experts in their field who knew more about their job than I did. The only thing for me to do was to give them full freedom and concentrate on the efficiency of the department. With a couple of people I also carried out some *real* research, leading to a publication in the prestigious journal *Polymer*. I firmly believed that it was the duty of the boss to understand his assistants, especially when it came to the yearly staff evaluation, and this drove me to learn Dutch more seriously.

Every year, Shell organised a meeting for managers of analytical departments in the various Shell locations, and our turn came around. Every session had a different chairperson, and because I was a manager in the host country I too had to chair a half-day session. When I started, I introduced myself and added that I felt like the Admiral in the Gilbert and Sullivan operetta *HMS Pinafore*. The Admiral's famous aria has a refrain whose gist, if not whose exact words, goes something like this: 'I never went to sea, but now I am the ruler of the Queen's navy.'

My direct boss was Aart van der Valk He was a good theoretical scientist, who later became a professor. He was also deeply religious. He didn't interfere with my work at all, which I liked. However, this was the only thing I liked about him. At the yearly evaluation, managers had to fill in two sheets. The first page contained details of each assistant's tasks for the year and comments about how they had been carried out, or, if not, why not. The boss had to write a short narrative, an appraisal of the assistant. The assistant had a right to see this, and there was a space provided where he could write his own comments, if he wished. Then there was a second page, which the assistant was not supposed to see, and this contained an evaluation of the assistant's long-term potential . It was a much more serious

Delft

evaluation of abilities such as creativity, imagination, analytical powers, etc. It ended with a recommendation on his career. Most bosses wrote nice things on the first page to avoid lengthy discussions and arguments, but the real criticism was reserved for the second page. When it was my turn to read the first page, written by him about me, the second page was lying beneath it, and halfway through the discussion Aart removed it and put it in his drawer.

'It's in the way,' he said by way of explanation.

The real reason was, of course, that the paper was so thin that with a little effort one might read what was written on the sheet below. His actions proved two things to me: he must have written very unpleasant things about me on the second page; and he had insulted my intelligence when he tried to justify himself. I always allowed my assistants to see both pages, but when I told my boss that I made a practice of doing this, he said it was specifically forbidden. 'OK,' I said, but the next time, in the middle of the discussion, with both sheets on the table, I suddenly had to 'go to the toilet.' Today, of course, all written information about a person must be open to him.

I represented Shell on a number of international committees, members of which met several times a year, always in a different location in Europe. We discussed the safe handling of our products, analytical methods, environmental issues and the like. To be honest, the best thing about them was the opportunity to travel to nice places, like Paris or Zurich. I accepted a job as project leader of a project designed to help the environment around the factories. I made suggestions for experiments, which were then carried out in one of our members' factories. I worked on it for years, but in the end I had to admit that it was a big and expensive failure. I still don't know why. We also had committees within the Shell group, where we discussed technological issues and decided on the research programme. Progress was always painstakingly slow. Committee members always came to a meeting representing the interests of their own function. This was in stark contrast to a project team, where every member was dedicated to the project. I think all committees should be abolished on the grounds that they are only wasting time....

The working atmosphere was friendly; everyone used given names and the familiar form of the pronoun 'you' when addressing each other. This appealed especially to the couple of Germans working in the laboratory, since back home they would use family names when addressing colleagues even after years of working together.

The following year I was elected to the work's council, or *Ondernemingsraad*, at KSPLD, which in Holland was required by law and whose work was regulated. Members had to be consulted by management before major decisions, and they had the right to veto certain changes affecting working conditions. Members were elected by vote, and the number of members depended on the number of employees. One year after my election, KSPLD and two more English laboratories were closed and their people offered jobs in Amsterdam 'to profit from a synergy between the different disciplines.' The old activities were to be continued in a newly built complex, but with far fewer people.

Our time in the work's council was taken up by negotiating with management over the transfer regulations and financial compensation offered by the company. I found the overall reduction in research activities bad for the future of the company and presented a graph to our management showing the amount of money spent on research by Shell as a percentage of the turnover in past years and extrapolated it into the future. The curve was approaching zero. I'd got the data from Shell's yearly financial reports, but it was not

Delft

appreciated by my director.

When it was announced that Carrington Plastic Laboratory was to be closed, the head of the analytical department there phoned me asking if he could come over for a discussion. I said yes, and promptly told my boss about our conversation. I didn't know the real reason for his visit, but I suspected that he wanted to see whether a good job vacancy might be available for him in Holland. On the day of the visit I got a telephone call from the director of the laboratory, Dr Goppel. They had obviously already decided on the new structure, and who would get what job.

'Did you know about this visit?' he asked.

'Yes,' I replied.

'And you didn't have the decency to tell this to your boss?' I specifically remember the word 'decency'. I was flabbergasted.

'But I *did*,' I said, after taking a deep breath. There followed a pause while he confronted my boss before continuing.

'Dr v.d. Valk is here, and he says you didn't.'

There was nothing more I could say. On his return from the management meeting, my boss felt he needed to put the record straight, so he said to me: 'Come to think of it, now I remember you *did* mention something....' But of course he didn't have the 'decency' to tell Dr Goppel. I consider this the worst thing a boss can do to a subordinate.

Now that my assignment in Holland was going to be longer than the two years originally planned, I wanted to buy my own house. Shell, however, was still not ready to finance this and only let us rent an unfurnished apartment and paid for the shipment of some of our own furniture from England. I could commute to Delft from the Hague by tram, so we decided to stay in the Hague. Another Shell expat had just bought a house, and his apartment was offered to us. The apartment was on the fifth floor and overlooked a nice park called, rather pretentiously, 'Little Switzerland'. We stayed in that flat for two years, by which time it was obvious that my home laboratory in England was scheduled to close down. We became permanently located in Holland and were able to sell our English house and buy one in Holland with financial help from Shell. We bought a house in Marlot, the most desirable part of the Hague. It was a big, old-fashioned house, but we loved to live there. I always used to say that if it wasn't for a few trees in the way we could overlook the residence of the Queen!

While I was working at Shell at Carrington, We received a Hungarian delegation, and I was asked to look after them. It soon became obvious to me that there were two graduate engineers, both speaking reasonable English, and one trustworthy comrade who spoke only Hungarian, and who was supposed to keep an eye on the two intellectuals. He reminded me of the manager of the Personnel Department in Almásfüzitő, where I had worked before, and I concentrated my attention on him. He was a simple man who turned out to possess one great skill: he could drink like a fish. During a buffet lunch, I pointed out to him that there was fresh salmon, something never seen in Hungary. Instead he chose to eat oily sardines straight from the tin, because he supposed this allowed him to drink more whisky. Fortunately we also had a salesman who could match his thirst, and the two of them finished a whole bottle of Scotch. I translated the discussion for him, which was conducted in English, but he was not really interested in all that. That evening we went to a nice country restaurant for dinner, and I helped him by explaining the menu and making

Delft

suggestions as to what to order. On the last day he gave me a box of Hungarian processed cheese which he'd brought with him, thinking that he'd have to rely on his own provisions in capitalist England . He was most grateful for my help and asked me naively, but with all sincerity: 'You are such a sympathetic person, may I call you comrade?' Of course, I agreed.

In Delft we had visitors from a Hungarian factory, making carpets from polypropylene fibres. The general manager, a big, jovial man, was accompanied by his chief production engineer. They used to come once a year at the invitation of Shell, as our guests. They were buying just enough polypropylene from Shell to qualify for a yearly visit and VIP treatment. I was asked to look after them and escorted them from the airport to the hotel. When they arrived and checked in, the first question they asked me was: 'Who pays for the hotel?' When I assured them that Shell would pay, their next question was: 'Will Shell tell our head office that they paid?'

'Of course not….'

This way, they could spend the cost of the hotel on presents for their families. Convertible currency was very much in short supply in Hungary. Had Shell told the truth, they would have had to return the money. I took them to our home for the rest of the afternoon and opened a bottle of white wine.

'How much did you pay for this house?' they asked, before the bottle was finished. I told them, and they immediately made a comparison with Hungarian house prices, converting the price into percentages of salaries. Next morning I collected them from the hotel and showed them around the laboratory. They were very interested in every new development concerning the application of the products, and in the machinery we used. Nothing escaped their attention, and they even noted the name on every drum of chemicals they saw lying around. Finally they made a suggestion: 'Would it be useful to Shell if they had a much larger pilot plant?'

'Sure, but it would be expensive to build and to operate.'

'Shell could use our factory as a pilot plant.'

We were taken aback by this offer. It was a good idea, but the time was not yet right to have such a 'joint venture' with a communist country.

On another visit, the production engineer suffered a heart attack and had to be taken to a hospital. After he was resuscitated he had to spend two more weeks recuperating. Shell paid all the expenses, including a visit by his wife from Hungary. Because she could speak only Hungarian and had no money on her, I had to go to the airport to assure the immigration officer that she was a guest of Shell. I also managed to get a small cash allowance for her on top of paying her hotel expenses at full board. I invited her to our home and learned that she was in fact Russian, but, being married to a Hungarian, she had learnt and spoke fluent Hungarian.

Walking in the Sauerland

Delft

In 1973, Vera and I celebrated our twenty-fifth wedding anniversary by having a winter holiday in that hilly region of Germany called the Sauerland. It was February, and everything was covered with deep snow. Most people were cross-country skiing, but we just walked in the hills. We liked it so much that we repeated it every following anniversary. Later on, Harry and Thea joined us, and we walked every morning to a different village, had a hot meal, and walked back to our hotel. After having a shower we played bridge till dinner. Walking in the snow required quite an effort, and later we changed our trip to Easter each year. We always stayed in the same small guesthouse, where they treated us almost as members of the family. The yearly outing continued for some twenty-five years, and only had to stop because Thea developed Parkinson's disease and couldn't walk.

The time for KSPLD to close was approaching, and we were busy to ensure that the work would continue in Amsterdam. The new organisation chart was approved, and according to this my new job was to lead a group responsible for process development in the chemicals from which plastic foams were made. Previously such a group hadn't existed, and all laboratory experiments were carried out in Egham, in a since-defunct laboratory. The people there were good theoretical chemists, but they had little practical experience and no knowledge of the manufacturing plant. I had to change this, which was an enormous challenge but one that also gave me a lot of satisfaction. One technician from Egham decided to accept a transfer to Amsterdam and joined my group; the rest of the people in my group were new to the job, and I considered this to be an advantage—to have an open mind is most important in research.

WHERE IS MY HOME?

Because of the closing down of the laboratory in Egham and the transferring of its activities to Holland, I had to travel a lot to integrate the work of the two laboratories. I was one day driving from work in Delft to Rotterdam airport, just a short distance, when to my horror I realised that I had left my passport at home. If I were to return and collect it, I would miss my plane. I decided to risk it and reported at the airport with my driving licence only, and they let me through. Fortunately I found several English colleagues of mine on the plane and I asked them to vouch for me on arrival in England. When I told the immigration officer my story, they all intervened, insisting: 'Not true! Don't believe a word of it!' I don't think there is another country in the world where they would have let me through, but in England they did. I made the journey back again, and in Amsterdam the frontier police said only: 'Welcome home.' But, of course, this was long before 9/11.

7
Amsterdam

SO WE HAD come to Amsterdam, this latest stop in our wanderings, and already this was the third city I had had to work in Holland. We had now lived in three countries, I had worked in six cities, but in spite of our efforts to integrate we still felt like foreigners everywhere we had been. Was this going to be the last stop, or would we have to move on again? Would we have a better chance at integrating and being accepted in Holland than in England? We would see. Shell offered new jobs to everyone working at KSPLD, but several people refused to move. They thought 80km was too great a distance and didn't want to leave their familiar environment.

Vera is often looking back into the past, and her biggest regret is still that we have only one son. She usually asks me if I regret anything, but I always insist that I don't. She doesn't regret leaving Hungary, but, given the choice, would we have also preferred to have stayed in one place instead of wandering across Europe? The honest answer is no. The world is a beautiful place, full of new experiences, and it would have been a great loss not to have met all the interesting people we did. Yet maybe there is one thing I regret—the fact that I can't show my emotions. I don't know why this is; certainly it's not by choice. Vera has long got used to it and accepts me as I am, but I'm sure that I've often given off the wrong signals to my son. I haven't praised him often enough, and I've never felt the need for bodily contact, like hugging him or kissing him. Is this because I was born under the sign of Aquarius? Or because I'm a logical-thinking scientist? I don't know.

The full name of the new laboratory was Koninklijke Shell Laboratorium Amsterdam, or KSLA for short. After my transfer there, for a while I commuted by train from the Hague. But the journey lasted over an hour each way, and I decided that it would be prudent to move nearer to Amsterdam. We had heard of a nice area of Holland called Het Gooi, the region round about the city of Hilversum, and once we had driven through it we immediately fell in love with its green woods, waterways, and pleasant-looking houses. We bought a house in Naarden, a 700-year-old city plundered by the Spanish in the sixteenth century. A few cannonballs are still preserved, embedded in the walls of its main church. After the Spanish had gone, an imposing fortification was built around the city, which is now a great tourist attraction. Again I made use of Shell's 100% mortgage guarantee and didn't sell our house in the Hague. Instead we let it, which provided us with a nice additional income. Because we liked the house, we thought that one day we might return to live there. Alas, after some 25 years we found its management too much of a burden and sold it.

The house we bought in Naarden was one end of a small, three-house terrace, and like most Dutch houses it had three storeys, one bathroom, and a small garden. What we liked most was that in front of it there were no houses but only a small stream and a tree nursery. Holland is full of these small canals, which take the ground water eventually to the sea in order to keep the low-lying country dry. The front of the house was covered with wooden panels, and all three houses were painted the same blue and white. It also had a garage for our car and garden utensils. It had three bedrooms on the first floor, and I converted the smallest of the three into my office while one of the two rooms on the second floor became my hobby-room.

We both liked antiques and often looked around in shops. One day we were looking at French pendulum clocks when a man of Indonesian origin stopped beside us

Amsterdam

and said he could point out the most beautiful one. To our surprise, his choice was a set of components in a shoebox. Seeing our shock, he said that he could build from these a very nice clock for a friendly price. It was rather cheap, and even adding on his fee it was still a bargain. I asked if I could join him and watch how he would set out to put the clock together. To be honest, I didn't completely trust him.

He lived in a flat and had a small room as a workshop, whose walls were covered with boxes of antique clock parts. If he found a part, such as a cogwheel, was missing, he searched for one from amongst his stock, carefully matching not only its size but also the number of teeth. It was tedious work and lasted a whole day, but the result was amazing. We still have and cherish that clock. I admired his work so much that I decided to take up clock making as a hobby and bought some tools and parts, which enabled me to do little repairs. I never became really good at it.

We had a widowed lady on each side as neighbours. One, Mrs Visser, was very self-sufficient, but the other, Mrs Knaap, felt lonely and frequently suffered from depression. We were very friendly with both of them, and I did small errands. Once, we suggested to Mrs Visser that she might occasionally invite Mrs Knaap over, because she was so lonely, but she proved uncharitable: 'Of course she's lonely! She's only been living here for fifteen years!'

Mrs Visser had been brought up on a farm and had learned to live a simple life. She was also exceptionally thrifty, even by Dutch standards. Occasionally she asked me to buy something for her at the supermarket, and when I delivered the goods and told her the price I had paid, she would take out a note from her purse.

'Have you got change?' she would ask. I found it amusing,

that I would have to count out the change into her hand before she was prepared to part with the note.

After four years in Holland we had a busy social life without having to wait the fifteen years. We had developed a special friendship with two Dutch couples. One of them was Joop, a chemist colleague at Shell, and his French wife. Jeannine was a small, highly intelligent woman with a university education, who was very patriotically French, uninterested in fashion, wore no make-up, and always dressed plainly. She was also an excellent cook and her signature dish was slices of ham embedded in sauerkraut and baked in a pastry shell. The other man, Luk, was Joop's childhood schoolmate, an insurance broker. His wife Dicky was just the opposite of Jeannine—tall, fashion-conscious, tastefully made-up, and with a job as a mannequin. Fortunately she too could cook, not so sophisticatedly perhaps, but still simple and tasty dishes. The six of us couldn't have been more different, but there was one common link: we all liked to eat and drink well, and we continued inviting each other in turn for gourmet dinners. There were always several courses with appropriate wines, and we would even produce menus showing what to expect. I honestly don't know when Vera learned to cook so well; certainly not from her mother! We had already started throwing dinner parties in England, Vera trying out all sorts of recipes. On our journeys abroad we collected lots of cookery books. But I think the most important factor was that she appreciated good food and liked to eat well.

As fate would have it, Joop developed cancer of the bladder, but instead of undergoing surgery he decided to try the 'Moerman Diet'. This was a very strict and sober diet, what might be called 'alternative medicine', developed by a Dutch doctor who had studied the effect of food on cancer. No more meat, sugar, coffee, or alcohol, but plenty of

Amsterdam

grains, fruit, and vegetables. The third couple immediately decided to stop with our dinner parties and dropped out of the loop, but we felt more compassionate. Next time they were due to come to us, Vera prepared a proper Moerman dinner for all four of us. It is still debated by doctors who are for and against alternative medicine whether this diet helped or not, but the fact remains that our friend lived happily and healthily for more than twenty years on this diet. As a result we too changed our eating habits, albeit not to the extent of the full Moerman prescription. Eventually Joop got depressed and tired of life, stopped his diet, and resumed eating as he had before his illness. The cancer soon returned, and after a year or so he died. Jeannine asked me to say a few words at his funeral, which I did.

Because István studied at the University of Edinburgh, we visited him by taking our car on the ferry from Europort to Hull. On one occasion we stopped in the beautiful city of York and admired the numerous antique shops. In one of the windows we saw a large oil painting of a flat landscape with a couple of farm workers holding a hoe and a rake. It reminded me of my hometown in Hungary, and we went inside. It had been painted in 1887 by one C. Shaw, and according to the information provided he had once been exhibited at the Royal Academy. It was a little too dark, and needed some cleaning, but we liked it and decided to buy it. At that time I still had my English bank account and chequebook, but I knew I had insufficient funds there to pay for the painting. So I made a suggestion to the shopkeeper: 'I can give you a cheque for the full amount, but don't try to cash it for a week, because first I have to transfer funds from Holland to my English bank. In the meantime I'll leaving the painting here, and when you've got the money please inform a friend of mine, who'll collect it.'

WHERE IS MY HOME?

I gave him the cheque and the name and address of an English colleague, who was soon to be transferred to Holland and could bring the painting together with his own belongings. I had started to walk out of the shop, when suddenly the man called out: 'Have you got your car with you?'

'Yes....'

'Then take the painting with you.'

Mrs Visser wouldn't have approved!

In my office

To accommodate the people transferred from the three laboratories that had been closed, a new building was hastily erected in KSLA to house polymer research. It used a lot of aluminium and plastics and had a modern design, almost

Amsterdam

futuristic, instantly recognisable amidst the rest of the old, sober structures. A new organisation was created which incorporated polymer research, but its people were insular and there was no sign of the much-discussed 'synergy' between the old and the new departments. I found this very interesting, because there is a lot of talk by management consultants about the 'management of knowledge'. To me this only proved that knowledge can't be managed; the most important ingredient is informal discussions, and this happens only between people who know each other.

The Personnel Department learned from past mistakes and invited the employees of those English laboratories which were closing for orientation, along with their wives. By this time I was a seasoned expatriate who knew what these people needed to know. I also knew, that they wouldn't get all the necessary information from the Personnel Department, so I wrote a small pamphlet giving them some practical advice about life and social customs in Holland, emphasizing the differences with England. Because I stated on the very first page that it was my personal view alone and didn't represent any official policy, Shell distributed it. It's a remarkable fact that a native of a country never notices those aspects of life which are so important to a foreigner who lives there. We are all so used to doing things the way we do, that we don't even contemplate that certain things can be different or done differently. I suppose it's a sort of snow-blindness.

A meeting was organised, where some seventy English people listened to various speakers, me amongst them. I told them what to expect, the good as well as the bad parts of expatriate life. I remember the sentence I started with: 'There are three billion people living in the world (this was in 1973!) and the great majority of them live "abroad". This proves that life outside England is possible.'

WHERE IS MY HOME?

I knew that most of these people would miss the hilly landscape of England, and tried to tell them that walking on the dunes in the north of Holland might give the impression of walking in Derbyshire. This statement was received with roars of laughter from the audience, and my credibility was lost. Later, however, a man who bought a house north of Amsterdam came to me saying: 'We love to walk in the dunes—now I can see why you compared them to Derbyshire.'

We again had a single canteen for most employees, except for the directors, who ate in a separate room. Their excuse was that they often continued their meetings during lunch, but I think the real reason was that they were treated a lot better there than the rest of us. It was interesting to observe a cultural difference between the Dutch and the English in the canteen: a Dutchman eating alone would select a corner and sit with his back to the wall, looking inward at the other people; an Englishman would also sit in the corner, but with his back to the room, facing the wall.

My new job was to improve the safety and efficiency of the manufacturing operation and to develop processes for new products. First I had to learn the existing process as it was employed in the plant at Pernis. During my training I was working with the operators as their shadow when one of them said to me: 'I've just hoisted the necessary three tons of raw materials up to the reactor, but two 50-kilo bags have been left out. Would you help me carry them up?'

I couldn't say no, so I put one bag on my back and started climbing the steps. By the time I reached the three-storey-high platform my legs were trembling and my whole body shaking. Of course the operator had done it on purpose, and had a good laugh at my expense.

Amsterdam

I found the plant at Pernis even more modern than those in England. The instrumentation especially was more advanced. The size of the operation was enormous, and there was a rigid and hierarchical management structure. The place was kept neat, with no rubbish lying around as sometimes happened in England and as was the norm in Hungary. Holland had an advanced system of technical education, and all shift foremen and most of the operators were very knowledgeable about their jobs. Returning to the laboratory, I concentrated on selecting our priorities and 'selling' the results to our customer, the manufacturing plant. I was lucky to have an excellent, well-trained, and motivated team. Because of the successes we achieved, I was promoted back to grade two, which I had had before I went to Holland, thereby probably becoming the only person in Shell to be promoted twice to the same grade. I wasn't unduly ambitious, but life within was just as competitive as between companies. I had started with a huge disadvantage, because I was already twenty-nine years old, while my colleagues were only twenty-two. Reaching a certain age, I was no longer considered for further promotion.

My direct boss was Brian G., a brilliant English scientist. He had also worked at Carrington and we were friendly with him and with his wife, but sadly she got cancer and died rather young. He had an excellent memory, and his Dutch vocabulary was more extensive than mine, yet he never spoke it; he felt that he could express himself correctly only in English. Brian had a cynical style and this upset a lot of his subordinates. Once he made a comment to me: 'No matter what you do, your project will be stopped next year.' Not exactly the right way to motivate your workers. I disagreed and made a wager, which I won. The prize was a bottle of whisky.

WHERE IS MY HOME?

In spite of the warning from Dan, my old English boss, that no job was secure, I completed twenty-five years' service with Shell and received my reward. Besides the badge with the tiny diamond, I got an extra month's salary and two weeks' extra holiday. What else could we do than go on a month-long tour of a lifetime? We started by travelling across Sri Lanka and continued with Singapore, Hong Kong, Bali, and Bangkok. It was like a dream, being in Asia for the first time, visiting Hindu and Buddhist temples, looking at monkeys in the wild, and at elephants working in the forests. Not surprisingly we got hooked on travel and did many more wonderful trips throughout the world.

Some of my team

The Dutch have an expression for a person who's always unlucky; they call him a *pechvogel* or 'bad luck bird'. David, my English assistant, who'd been transferred to Holland, was a typical example of a *pechvogel*. He was a slow but accurate worker, paying a great deal of attention to safety,

Amsterdam

and I soon found the best job for him. I put him in charge of lab safety and he had to train all the new assistants. He and his wife bought a house in the north of Holland, and every day David took the train to work. But because house prices were much higher in Holland they could only afford a small, terraced home. These were built with pre-fabricated concrete and were notorious for transmitting noise through their structure. As expected, Jill couldn't sleep. There was only one solution; the sound-proofing in the bedroom had to be improved by building a room *inside* the room and filling the space in between with sound-insulating material. For a while, everything was fine, but as time went on, the noise in the new 'inner' bedroom started to increase again. Jill went to bed one night but remained wide awake and suddenly sat up shouting to her husband: 'I can still hear it!' She couldn't sleep anymore; she had to remain awake all night to listen to the noise. David wore his cross quietly, without complaint. He worked at his steady space and made a useful contribution to the success of our team. Whenever we completed a project, after it was proven commercially we organised a party to celebrate. I always invited all my assistants and also those from other departments who had contributed to the success. We used to have such parties at least twice a year and it greatly contributed to the good working atmosphere. The departmental budget however allowed one party only and I and my graduate assistants would pay for the consumption of others in a public bar. David never came to these parties. At first, he gave some transparent excuses, but later he had to admit the truth. If he didn't get the train he was meant to and was more than fifteen minutes late home, Jill threw his dinner into the bin. This happened even if the train was genuinely delayed for some reason.

WHERE IS MY HOME?

Once David had an important experiment which he didn't finish on time, and so he asked for permission to come in and work over Christmas, when almost everything was closed. Because nobody was allowed to work alone, I volunteered to come in and keep him company.

'That's what a boss is for,' I said to my complaining wife. It was a cold winter, and we found the radiators rather cold too. Our laboratory was on the top floor, so we thought that there was air in the system which had to be vented off. David couldn't find the key, so he set about with a spanner. In no time he'd broken off the whole valve and hot water from the radiator had started to flood the room. We stuffed the hole with rags and phoned the technical service unit, but it was Christmas and they were understaffed. Eventually they came and repaired it, but we had to spend the rest of Christmas Day cleaning the floor. Then on another occasion David discarded some chemicals into a steel drum we kept in the lab for collecting material for destruction. Later in the day he also emptied the contents of a small glass vessel which, unfortunately, also contained some catalyst residues. The drum was closed, and we all went home. Next morning we found that the catalyst had activated the rest of the chemicals, a lot of heat had been generated, and the lid of the steel drum had been duly blown right up into the ceiling, bending several aluminium panels. In spite of all these mishaps, everybody liked David because of his quiet and polite style.

I was elected for a second time to a works council, this time at KSLA. I was very proud to have come eighth from a total of seventeen. This was a particularly large council, since there were 2,200 people employed there at the time. I cannot deny the fact that a large English vote helped me to win this position. Again we were involved with extensive reorganisation and slimming down.

I had a difficult time on the council. It was a time of economic recession and increasing unemployment, and the council members who were affiliated to a trade union wanted to talk about nothing else but work-sharing. They were advocating, nay demanding, shorter working hours for those with jobs, so that more people could be employed. I was a free member, without union affiliation, and tried very hard to convince them that such an act would lead to inefficiencies. I even wrote an article, published in a Dutch weekly, suggesting that instead of working shorter hours we should work harder and longer to become more competitive with Asia. On the other hand, I was also at the same time arguing with the management, whom I found unduly secretive and authoritarian.

You might have gathered by now that I was not a man without prejudice. I was not very fond of personnel departments and their managers. I also objected to the name 'Human Resource Management'. I felt that I was George Pogany, not a 'human resource'. When the manager of the Personnel Department at KSLA retired, as was customary his secretary approached all senior staff for a contribution to his farewell book and for his leaving present. I gave her an empty sheet with just my signature, in the centre of which I had placed a 5c coin. I'm not sure if the sheet was ever placed in his book, as I didn't go to his farewell party.

I have always liked to write, and throughout my career I had several scientific publications, but later I changed topics and started publishing about managerial work. I even got a congratulatory letter from an American publisher, Marcel Dekker, for an article in the journal *Chemtech* entitled 'You can still go wrong using statistics'. I also had about seven patents to my name, but according to my work contract I sold the rights to Shell in return for a payment of just $1 each. This never bothered me; I did my work because I liked it and wanted to be successful. A Nobel Prize is the highest award for fundamental research, but granting a patent is the highest recognition of industrial research. I must admit, though, that some of my patents were useless and that we did it just to keep competitors off the scent.

I still liked to listen to the BBC World Service and enjoyed its short stories. They used to ask listeners who were living abroad to submit short stories with a local flavour, and one day I sent in mine, the story of Gizi. She had been my colleague at university, had got involved in an extramarital affair, and had committed suicide using cyanide with its distinct smell. The BBC accepted it with two minor modifications and changed the title from 'The smell of bitter almonds' to just 'Bitter almonds.' As a chemist I didn't really think this was correct, because the story was not about almonds, but it did make the title short and crisp. They also changed my description of her 'beautiful breasts' to 'beautiful shoulders.' I found this childish. Most men can acknowledge a beautiful woman's breasts, but how do you distinguish between beautiful or ugly shoulders? I'm sure today's editors would stick with the breasts! The BBC paid me £47 for this 'unsolicited communication' and sent me a schedule of the broadcast times. The first was in the middle of the night, but we were wide awake and I made a tape-recording of it. The second was soon after midday, and I decided to make use of our lunch break and invited a number of my colleagues to listen to it 'with coffee and cakes'. I took a portable radio and set it up in the conference room, ordered cakes from the local shop, and got coffees at 5c each from the machine. Some thirty people came, and after listening to the story I proudly accepted their congrat-

Amsterdam

ulations. About two years later the BBC repeated the broadcasts and again paid me £47.

In 1984 I bought my first computer, an English made 'BBC'. It had a tiny memory of a mere 28 kilobytes and a word processor on a chip. I was not interested in programming or in computer science, but I recognised its benefits in writing and was aware of the need to become acquainted with this new technology. I can't understand how intelligent older people, including some scientists, proudly say that they have no interest in computers, as if someone two hundred years ago would have boasted that he had no interest in learning to read and write.

This just about sums up my professional career as a chemist. In the meantime my basic knowledge had gone out of date and the topics on which I had worked were the property of Shell. I had become fully dependent on my employer, so it came as a shock when in 1983 Shell decided to reduce their research budget and shed some four hundred personnel from their Amsterdam laboratory by asking for voluntary early retirement with financial compensation. This was a painful decision for all those, including myself, who had spent years working on various projects. I wrote a critical paper with the title 'Cutting back on research; is it good business?' and sent it to a British journal, who published it under the pseudonym 'Dr Gap'. A month later I was approached by a Canadian businessman who had liked my article. We ended up visiting each other in Holland as well as in Canada.

To achieve the reduction without sacking people, Shell offered a generous redundancy package to everyone over fifty. The actual termination of employment was scheduled for the end of 1985, and they asked for volunteers. The compulsory retirement age was sixty, so most people over

WHERE IS MY HOME?

fifty-five accepted the offer and Shell lost a vast amount of knowledge and experience. My predictions proved to be correct, and eventually Shell did reduce their activities in chemicals and sold out or did away with the whole of its plastics business.

I liked my work, and my team and I considered ourselves successful. I didn't want to go, and the pressure I felt caused me a lot of stress. It was time to pay for the luxuries of expatriate life. I had joined Shell in England, and my pension was based on my nominal English salary, which was some 20% lower than the equivalent Dutch salary, while the expatriate allowance also was excluded. While most Dutch employees received about 80% of their final salary as a pension, in my case it was only 50%. Several years earlier I had asked for this to be changed and to be put on the permanent staff of the Dutch laboratory, but the management refused to grant me a full Dutch pension.

The author on his retirement from Shell

Amsterdam

To achieve their aim, Shell used the carrot-and-stick method. Besides the generous financial package, they made life rather unpleasant for those people they wanted to get rid of. They changed my title from 'section head' to simply 'head', indicating less responsibility. There were hints that I might have to share my office with someone. When I met one of the younger departmental heads she asked me bluntly: 'Why don't you just go?' It was obvious that I wasn't wanted anymore. Eventually I too signed the papers agreeing to early retirement. Now it was no longer an uncertainty, and at the age of fifty-eight I started to make plans for my future.

At my farewell party I made a speech, evaluating this time not my assistants but my bosses. I was bitter and cynical, and made comments I now regret. In evaluating people, Shell often used the expression 'helicopter ability', meaning they had a wide view of things. In evaluating my boss, Brian, I now used the term 'submarine ability', implying that he was staying on while I had to resign. It was most unfair of me.

8

Training managers.

IT IS A painful fact that nobody is indispensable. I had thought that my accumulated experience would be utilised even after I had left and was expecting an occasional telephone call from members of my ex-team with questions. At least, I'd thought, they would be discussing their plans with me and asking for my comments. None of this happened, and I should have known better. Shell employs ambitious people who feel that, once they are in charge, there is no need for anybody else. I had to look elsewhere to keep my mind occupied.

My first idea was to work at a university in England, as an industrial fellow with no salary, but with access to certain facilities—the library and so on. I was hoping that this would also provide us with a reasonable social life. I would have loved to go back to Oxford, but I knew that there was little chance of that. I went to the University of Buckingham, a new university near Oxford, and talked to a professor there. He received me with much courtesy, but didn't reply to my formal letter. This reinforced my conviction that industry and academe would never truly mix.

I was approached by a head-hunter who suggested that I should join Van Leer, a Dutch company, makers of steel and plastic drums, whose boss wanted someone to manage their department of material science. This forced us to make an important decision. Under my contract with Shell, they had to repatriate us to England, pay all removal expenses, and reimburse the costs of selling and buying a house. Financially I would have been better off in England in the long run, because of the lower rate of taxation. But on the other side of the coin there were three arguments for staying in Holland: (i) our health cover was better in Holland, and at our age we couldn't expect to get decent, private insurance in England; (ii) we had a lively social life in Holland, while our old English friends were now scattered all over the country. István lived in England, yes, but we decided not to become a burden on him; (iii) I had something useful and profitable to do in Holland, at least for a while.

We decided to stay, and I accepted the Van Leer offer and signed a contract for one year with a very attractive salary. I was working not only in a new city now, but also, after twenty-eight years with Shell, at a new company. The material science 'department' I was heading consisted of me and a metallurgist, who turned out to be an ethnic Hungarian from Romania. He was not Jewish, but was married to a Jewish girl, and they had both come to Holland via Israel. As it happened, he was more Jewish in his behaviour than his wife, spoke Hebrew, and occasionally acted as interpreter for the local rabbi, who couldn't speak Hebrew!

Van Leer had several factories, mainly in the proximity of their customers in the petrochemical industries, so that empty drums didn't have to be transported over long distances. The research laboratory was on a separate site, and every morning I would drive there on a picturesque route along the waterways. All through the summer they were full of beautiful, yellow water-lilies. In the winter the road became treacherous with ice, and the scenery reminded me of Jan Steen's painting, *Winter Landscape*. In the laboratory, eighty people worked on widely diverse applications, from steel drums through to plastic drums, plastic sheets, and paper drums, each led by an experienced department head. There were far too many projects to be handled effectively by the staff.

My career at Van Leer turned out to be a mismatch. I knew what material science was, but my boss had a very different idea. He wanted someone with knowledge of the commercially available polymers, their properties, prices, limitations, etc. My knowledge was more useful to the makers of these products than to their end-users. After a year and a quarter my contract was terminated. I must confess that I was very upset about my short stay at Van Leer. I considered myself a better-trained, more creative scientist than the rest of them and had never looked at myself as a failure. I was having nightmares about it for a time. I think one of the biggest problems was that the permanent staff was not used to working in teams. I was supposed to function as an adviser, but nobody ever came to me for advice, and, when I gave it, people considered it interference and didn't take it. They might also have resented my high salary. Company cultures can be as diverse as national cultures.

I had one more idea about what I could do with myself. In my last years at Shell I had been not so much a chemist as a manager, and I thought I might train young scientists in the art and science of management. As my time at Shell was coming to an end, I had written offering my services as a lecturer to Intermediair Training, a Dutch management-training organiser, and also to the International Management Institute (IMI) in Geneva, among others. I had had encouraging replies from both. A man named Emil, who was already giving research management courses for Intermediair, asked me to perform as his guest speaker. Emil was a tall, slim, immaculately dressed, middle-aged man with several years' experience working in the research department of a Swedish company. He was also an excellent and experienced trainer, always thinking big, and asking top price for his work.

I wanted to make my contribution as sophisticated as possible and included a subject which was new to me as

WHERE IS MY HOME?

well. It was a disaster. People asked me questions I couldn't answer, and Emil wanted to stop me contributing anything more. I had to beg him to give me another chance, and realised that I mustn't talk about anything except from personal experience. Eventually we did have several years of pleasant co-operation, and were mutually complementary. He used to call our partnership 'sugar and vinegar' (I was the sugar), implying, or rather acknowledging, his own provocative style. This style went down well with some of the participants, but others, especially women, hated it.

My work at IMI had had a dramatic start. To my letter, I had had a reply from Michael, an Englishman, who led the course entitled 'Research Management.' He wrote that he was interested in meeting me and to look him up if ever I was in Geneva. As it happened, I got his letter on a Friday, and I had to attend a meeting in Zurich on the next Monday, representing Shell on an international committee. I phoned Michael asking for an appointment late on Monday. He was free, and at Amsterdam airport I changed my ticket from Zurich–Amsterdam to Zurich–Geneva–Amsterdam. I'm not sure if I would ever have invested in the full airfare just to get to this interview. Michael started testing my knowledge and my views on research management. I probably gave all the right answers, and once I mentioned that, in my view, speed was very important and that I called this a 'research *blitzkrieg*'. He liked this expression so much that he got up, shook my hand, and said that his middle name was also George. I was in. He said that the reason for the success of TV soaps like Dallas was that every fifteen minutes viewers got a shock, and he asked me to send him some 'shock statements' which I'd be using in my work. I did this, and he invited me to give a half-day seminar on 'the human aspects of research management' at the next course, in Geneva. I was to have all my expenses paid, plus a fat cheque.

Training Managers

I was excited, knew my subject, and thought that this time nothing could go wrong. I prepared a few handwritten overhead slides using different-coloured pens, and gave a rather formal lecture, more like a speech from the pulpit—dry, monotone, and uninteresting. Afterwards, Michael told me it had been very bad.

'Do you really want to continue with this work?' he asked.

'More than anything else,' I replied. Because the participants judged the *content* of my lecture, at least, very important, he gave me a second chance. I realised that a training course had to be interactive, quite different from the straight talks I had given at Shell. In fact, a good trainer had to be a good entertainer, and participants had to enjoy the course. I would even go as far as to say that, for some of them, learning was a secondary aim. Apart from the 'shock statements', I had to tell jokes relevant to the subject, design and run various management games, organise group discussions, and so on. I approached our own training manager at Shell, and asked him to coach me in the art of giving an interactive seminar. It cost me a bottle of whiskey, but it turned out to be a good investment. I also asked Michael to allow me to listen to their star lecturer, Professor Tom Allen from MIT, and I learned a lot from him. I was lucky as well in that the next IMI seminar was organised in Finland, and the Finns are ethnically related to the Hungarians. From the start there was a special relationship between the participants and myself, and at the evaluation I scored better than Tom Allen. Michael was satisfied. I must confess, though, that this outcome was unjust, and that I never reached the excellence of Tom.

IMI was very commercially minded and would not run a course unless there were over thirty participants. This reduced the possible interaction, and playing certain management games became very difficult. Sometimes there was more conflict within one group of negotiators than between the negotiating parties. The alternative was to run the games in parallel, which often led to confusion. One negotiating game, developed by Professor Mastenbrook, involved four companies of builders, who had to acquire certain parcels in exchange for others. Students used to solve this in fifteen minutes by collecting all the information on who owned what and who needed what, and realised that by simple exchanges this can all be achieved. Without full knowledge of all the data, the exchange was more difficult, because it always had to go via a third party. There would also be a certain amount of irrelevant and misleading information, and middle-managers needed about an hour to solve the problem. But given a very competitive environment consisting of *top* managers, even two hours was not enough. They were so secretive; they didn't want to reveal what they owned and what they needed to buy. I asked one of them, the research director of a large, multinational company: 'Why did you just buy that piece of land, when you don't need it?'

'To mislead them,' he answered with a wink.

Well, he succeeded; I had to stop the game unfinished to be able to catch my aeroplane home.

IMI advertised me in their brochures as an 'Ex-Process Development Manager at Shell'. Strictly speaking I was only one of such managers, and the description could be misunderstood by inserting 'the' instead of 'a'. This attracted the attention of the co-ordinator of research at Shell, and through the director of the laboratory he requested that I remove the reference to the company. I rememberd the Latin proverb *aquila non captat muscas*, 'the eagle doesn't catch flies'. Either he's not an eagle or I'm not a fly, I thought. I informed Michael, and he ignored it. In all, I made a dozen

Training Managers

trips to Geneva, two to Finland, and participated in several courses given by IMI in Holland. A few times I took Vera with me, and we spent the weekends in a small hotel on the top of one of the Swiss mountains. The pay for half a day's work was enough to cover all our expenses. Eventually IMI merged with another Swiss training organisation and had no more need for my services.

Having worked for IMI provided me with an excellent reference and opened the door to several organisations. One of them had a good reputation for providing management training courses in Holland. First I was invited to give a contribution to a course for expatriates and their wives, called 'Know the Netherlands'. I talked about the culture shock and social customs in Holland. My personal examples and the numerous anecdotes and jokes were very much appreciated. However, my very conscientious Dutch boss got upset when I said that in Holland it was customary to give cash as presents on a birthday or anniversary. She thought that this put Dutch people in a bad light and asked me not to say it any more. Well, it was true that giving cash wasn't compulsory, as some people took flowers, alcohol, or bonbons, but in order to avoid receiving twenty bunches of flowers the usual thing was to prepare a list of desirable items. At the top of the list was almost always an envelope with cash in. I repeated the story at the next course, and she duly removed me from her list of trainers. This was not the first nor the last time that sticking to my guns caused me financial disadvantage, but I had no regrets and would do it again.

The training courses at the organisations I worked for were usually held in large, country hotels, in the middle of some woods, far away from large cities. A course usually lasted three days, from 9am till 7.30pm, followed by a drink at the bar and then dinner. I would have to stand all the time and walk between people, occasionally sitting on the edge of my table. I also had to be alert, answering questions and concentrating the whole day, until about 10.30pm when dinner ended and I could return to my room, dead tired.

The author leading a training course

Shell had two training organisations, one for graduates already in management jobs, and one for the middle cadre. The first was held in English and employed trainers from well-known companies with international reputations. The second was held in Dutch, and I got a job leading a five-day training course called 'Middle Management.' My personal experience of the way Shell worked enabled me to use lots of real-life stories and examples. This was a great asset, and I was always given ridiculously high ratings by the participants. I worked for several years, giving half a dozen courses a year, until one day a new boss took over at the top and the whole organisation was suddenly closed down.

Training Managers

'Until now we've decided what people should be learning,' they said at the last meeting. 'From now on we'll be providing what they ask for. Like doctors, we'll wait for someone to come to us with a health complaint.'

'This reminds me of my Hungarian army doctor,' I said. 'If a soldier came to him with a complaint concerning his body above the belt, he got aspirin. If the complaint was below the belt, he got a laxative. I think training should be tailor-made to individual requirements, and the trainer's in a better position to judge what they are than a young manager.'

But it was no use, and the new boss of Shell had already decided on closure. The whole organisation and all its equipment were dismantled. Nobody came with requests to be trained because, most managers don't know that they need to know. It was simply a short-sighted, cost-saving exercise.

I was invited to be the guest speaker on a general management course held by a reputable organisation, which was less successful. I found it difficult to talk rationally about decision-making to non-technical people. I'm convinced that accountants and technicians think differently. I listened there to another speaker, an American professor, a very good and popular lecturer. He wore black shoes, dark-blue trousers, and a short-sleeved white shirt with a fancy tie. He also sported not only a golden watch but also a thick, gold chain on his wrist. He was not a young man, but instead of walking he would run amongst the participants. Hi took just five minutes, and he told everyone that he had his own company worth $25m. Not my style.

Because of the difficulties in training non-technical people I realised that I had to stick to training exclusively technicians and developed a most successful course called 'The Technical Manager'. It ran for some fifteen years under the title 'Leading Technical Personnel'. My greatest asset once again was the many lived examples I could use to support the theory. I was always very keen in pointing out the difference between theory and practice. 'In theory,' I used to say, 'I can play tennis very well. I know that I have to pull my hand back in order to give the ball a hard hit. In practice, however, I always miss the ball.'

One of my most successful seminars was 'Technical Report Writing in English', and I gave it to several large Dutch companies, in all some fifty times. My English was not perfect, and I had to brush up my knowledge of grammar, but the participants knew even less. With the introduction of improved word-processing software with its grammar- and spell-check, the demand for this course suddenly disappeared. This was a pity, because I had looked in detail at many aspects of a technical report not covered by such software, such as style, structure, and the credibility of the writer as a salesman for his ideas. I always asked each participant to send me in advance a report written by him, and I read them and gave my comments. 'The reader might not be as knowledgeable on the subject as you are, but never underestimate his intelligence,' I would comment.

To be successful, there must be a bond between the trainer and his participants. If the participant dislikes the trainer, he'll dislike his subject as well. Just as in the theatre, people value the training according the worst thirty seconds. The worst situation I ever experienced was when a junior worker with a small brain and a big mouth attended with his boss. Junior wanted to prove to his boss how critical he was, and he didn't stop asking stupid questions. He was never satisfied with the answer, and at the end he gave me a very low rating while his boss gave an '8'. Fortunately this happened only once.

Training Managers

I applied to an advertisement asking for part-time teachers for an American university in Leiden. I got the job, but their contract only ever covered a single course stretched over eight weeks, at one evening per week from six till ten, because the students were all working adults. The contract had to be renewed for every subsequent or new course. The general framework of the subject was given, but there was considerable latitude for each teacher, which I liked. I taught undergraduates for a BA degree, later also postgraduates, and, later still, I contributed to an MBA course. My subject was 'Business Policies & Strategies'. This was the last course of the MBA, and it pulled together everything the students had studied in the previous two years. Personally I don't believe in exams. With the availability of computers and search engines, memory is not as important as it used to be, so I would ask the students to prepare a business plan instead and submit it at the end of the course. Every one of them suffered from the same mistake of being much too optimistic.

Grading the students was a serious problem, and I maintained that there was no way one could grade objectively. There were teachers who considered the amount of work a student produced as the basis for the grade. I thought that the most important question was: 'will this person perform as expected in real life?' I considered that my customers were not the students, nor the University, but instead the industrial and commercial organisations who eventually employed them as graduates. Would *they* be satisfied? Another aspect of grading was that one always made a subconscious internal ranking in any given class: in a class full of excellent students, the average got a lower grade than he would have in a class of poor students. Why was a grade so important to the students anyway? Nobody would ever ask them what grade they had received for a specific subject. It was simply a way of introducing competition at the expense of real learning. They didn't dare to argue their case against the opinion of the teacher, because they thought it would be held against them, even though in my case the opposite was true. Regrettably they didn't always believe me.

Some of the students were excellent, others less so. I got the impression that many of them, especially those already working as accountants, were more interested in getting a degree and less in learning new skills. Once, the director asked me to tutor a student who needed one course only to complete his studies. I agreed, on condition that the student came to my home instead of me going to Leiden. The student arrived in a huge, black BMW with tinted windows, and his driver stayed in the car during the tutorial. He was a young man in a sporty outfit, working for his father's business as marketing director. Vera was most impressed and brought us coffee and biscuits in our best Herend china. We discussed a few relevant topics, and I wanted to give him some homework, but he protested that he had very little time. Still, I needed some to check his communication skills.

'Have you read any management books?' I asked him. He named one, which I also had sitting on my shelf. 'Write a short essay on this book. What did you learn from it?' Next week he arrived again in his BMW but he didn't bring an essay. 'What do you remember from our discussion last week?' I asked.

'Nothing,' was his short but honest answer.

'If you think that you can buy a degree here, you're at the wrong address,' I told him. 'I believe there are markets in Asia where you can,' I concluded, and sent him home.

Training Managers

I'm rather proud of the fact that I never missed an appointment. In all, I worked over twenty-two years as a trainer, in eight countries, using three languages, and I enjoyed every minute of it. I was my own boss, and if I made a mistake (and I did a few) I could blame nobody but myself. In the beginning I tried to do too much, thinking that all my knowledge and experience had to be transferred to the participants. Later I realised that I had to trim the message and concentrate more on the entertainment. It is fair to say that I too developed the style of an entertainer, fishing for compliments and appreciation. I considered this a more welcome reward than the money, which was nevertheless exceptionally good. When I saw that people were taking notes, asking questions, enjoying a game, I felt on the top of the world. I always received applause at the end of a course, and occasionally I also got a present from the grateful participants, like a bottle of wine or a plant for Vera. An additional benefit of working abroad was that I could take Vera with me. I had to pay for her expenses, like travel and hotels, but I could afford it on my income and we often spent the weekend in a nice place after the course had concluded. Vera occasionally liked to go with me to a Dutch hotel, to enjoy a luxurious bathroom and beautiful surroundings for a pleasant change.

Eventually I had to stop, partly because the competition from younger people became more pressing and partly because I never advertised. I also grew old, and the examples I used from experience became dated. Young participants looked at my white hair and decided that my knowledge was no longer up to date. I think they were wrong. Human nature, my main subject, hadn't changed in the last twenty-two years, but perception is often more important than the truth. In the end, the customer, as they say, is always right.

WHERE IS MY HOME?

Having more time on my hands, I decided to rewrite the pamphlet I had prepared to help my English colleagues and their families settle into Holland, and turned it into a book. My Hungarian uncle created some illustrations, and I gave it the title *How to be Happy in Holland*. Two thousand five hundred copies were printed in 1995, and all were sold in bookshops. My main message was that foreigners had to integrate into their new environment in order to be happy, but need not fully assimilate. In fact, an adult can't assimilate, and only a young child can. Yet there is no problem in being different, as long as we accept each other as equals. I received many comments about my book, all positive, including a review in one of the Dutch daily papers. Originally I had thought that companies with a large number of expatriates would buy the book for their staff, but none of them did. Even when I sent them a copy, personnel depart-

Training Managers

ments were not interested. If only they had asked their expatriate workers!

Shell had a shop at the laboratory in Amsterdam selling candles, paper serviettes, soap, etc. I went there one day with a copy of the book.

'I can give you ten copies,' I said to the manager. 'You don't have to pay now, just stock them on a shelf. I'll give you a 30% discount on the cover price, and what you don't sell I'll take back. I have a registered company, so I can give proper invoices.'

'I'll have to discuss it with my boss,' he said.

I knew what the outcome would be, because his boss was the manager of the Personnel Department. After about a month I received an official 'no.'

At our golden wedding anniversary, we gave a party, held at a nice country restaurant. We employed a string quartet, and they were there before the guests arrived, greeting them with soft, pleasant music. We had the compulsory champagne reception and a three-course meal. Besides our Dutch friends, we had our son over, my brother-in-law and his wife from Canada, and six couples from England. The party was a memorable day, but we didn't repeat it ten years later, mainly because in the meantime so many of the people there had become ill or had died, amongst them István wife, Ruth. Because of her poor health they had no children, and consequently we have no grandchildren. This is a cause of great sadness to Vera, who loves children and who, because of my own cool nature, showers her affection instead on our small dog. Her favourite bread is cairn terriers, little but alert, with a black patch around the mouth and the ears and tail always pointing up.

As is customary in Holland, the mayor of our city wanted to congratulate us on the day of our sixtieth anniversary,

WHERE IS MY HOME?

The mayor congratulates the Pogánys on their anniversary

but we were in Egypt snorkelling. He came a week later with a bunch of flowers and a photographer, and next week there was an article in the local paper under the headline 'Snorkelling on their 60th wedding anniversary.' They found it hilarious. We also got a congratulatory letter from the Queen of the Netherlands.

István, who has been living in England all the time we have been in Holland, hasn't spoilt us with his presence, and he finds it enough if he calls once a week, most of the time when in a hurry. On one of his visits we took him to a nice lake nearby, where we hired a rowing boat. We were paddling along, just like we once had on the Danube, when we met a small motorboat with a 'for sale' sign. We were invited aboard and my son enthusiastically proclaimed: 'Why don't you buy it, dad? Then I'd come over to visit you more often.' Everybody else warned me not to buy a boat without being sure that I like the idea of water sports.

Training Managers

'First hire a boat for a week, and then you'll know if it's for you,' they said. I thought that was a waste of money, so next spring I bought an 8m-long motorboat and we're still getting a lot of pleasure from it. As a matter of fact, I am writing this sentence while sitting aboard it in a marina. My son, though, doesn't visit us any more often, but he too has bought a Canadian canoe and uses it on rivers and estuaries in England. I thought I knew how to sail a boat; after all, I used to have a kayak on the Danube, and I can drive a car, so I took the boat out of its box at the marina and pottered around the lake without any problem. Returning it to the narrow box was another matter. I had to shout and ask for help until someone in a rubber boat helped me back in. I realised that I needed tuition and phoned a school, who sent me a teacher.

'I've no problem manoeuvring the boat on the lake,' I told him. 'My problem is that I can't get it back into its box.'

'No, sir,' the teacher said. 'Your problem is that you don't know how to sail a boat.'

WHERE IS MY HOME?

And of course he was right. I took four lessons, and after some experience I can now claim that I have full control over the boat. Every year we can hardly wait for spring, to get into the boat and sail for several weeks around the beautiful waterways of Holland. We find that simply gazing at the water is relaxing; it soothes the nerves. Not only does the Dutch countryside look more attractive from the water, but our fellow boatpeople are also much more helpful than drivers on the road. Whenever we want to stop, those already moored come to our aid without asking. Vera throws a rope to them, and they pull the boat to the shore. There is no feeling of competitiveness, as you find on the roads. Life can be beautiful even after retirement.

9

Visiting Hungary.

THE COMMUNISTS called the Hungarian Uprising of 1956 'counter revolutionary' and punished those who actively participated in it. The fact that we had left Hungary without permission was also considered to be a crime, but after some six years had passed they pronounced a general amnesty on that score. From then onwards it was safe to go back, unless there was a warrant for your arrest because of your role during the revolution. I knew they had nothing against me or Vera, but still we didn't trust them.

It took us sixteen years before we worked up enough courage to go back and visit Hungary. By this time we had our British passports, but we still didn't take our twenty-year-old son with us in case he was recruited into the Hungarian army. We got a visa from the Hungarian embassy in the Hague, and knowledgeable people told us that this guaranteed safe exit from, as well as entry into, the country. It was 1973, Hungary was still communist, but, as people jokingly called it, it was 'goulash communism'. It meant that Hungary obediently followed the external policies of the Russians, but, perhaps in exchange, they were allowed more freedom in their local economy. This was in stark contrast to the way Romania worked under Ceaușescu. We had to change a certain amount of foreign currency at the official exchange rate for every day we wanted to spend in Hungary. Import and export of the Hungarian *forint* was forbidden, but there was a lively black market for currency exchange, giving at least twice that of the official rate.

I couldn't stop thinking about my return to Hungary after the war and tried to compare my feelings. Then I had come penniless, looking for my lost childhood, bitter about what they had done to me and not knowing what to expect. Now I was termed by the regime 'a fellow patriot who drifted away', and was very much welcome. But was it really me they were welcoming, or the hard currency I brought with me? In 1945 I had thought I would stay in Hungary forever; now I knew that after a fortnight I would be returning home to Holland.

It was late and we had no fixed address to go to in Budapest, so we decided to spend a night at Visegrád, a popular Danube town with the ruins of a fortress. We wanted to make a telephone call to our relatives in Budapest, and asked a passer-by where we might find a post office or a telephone kiosk. He looked at us as if we had come down from the moon and said at a surprised voice: 'But it's gone 4pm!' We took this to mean that it was so late in the afternoon that there was no such service available anywhere. Eventually we found a small hotel and checked in. There were no en-suite rooms, and to our disgust we found the communal toilet blocked and foul-smelling. I approached the fat lady sitting at the desk, smoking a cigarette. She didn't look at me but just continued talking to another person, probably the cook. I interrupted her.

'Do you know that the toilet's full, and blocked?'

'I know,' she said, and remained at her desk, smoking and talking away.

We wanted to have dinner in the restaurant and found a menu typed on a sheet of paper. It had several attractive dishes listed, and we had started to discuss the merits of *vadas hús* as against *borjú pörkölt* when the waitress interrupted: 'There's only *bableves* and *lekváros palacsinta*.' Was it to be bean soup, or pancakes with jam…? After dinner, Vera asked for a cup of tea, while I wanted a latté.

'We have only *dupla*,' answered the waitress. *Dupla* is Hungary's short and strong espresso.

'You do have hot water? Put a tea bag into it.'

'We have hot water, but no tea bags and no milk.'

Visiting Hungary

Even in expensive restaurants and coffee shops we couldn't get any tea or coffee with milk, because no Hungarian would ever ask for them and the tourist industry hadn't yet started.

Working ethics hadn't changed very much. Going over bad road surfaces, my car seat broke, but fortunately I found a large garage with a workshop nearby. I drove in, but nobody paid any attention to me because they were having a break, and instead of coffee or tea most of the workers were drinking beer. Eventually I'd had enough of waiting and told Vera rather loudly in Hungarian: 'With so many people here, I don't know who I should give the tip to….' That did it, the seat was welded in no time, and we could continue our journey.

In Budapest we stayed cheaply at a private address we'd got from the tourist office. It was in the centre of the city, we had a nice room with a separate entrance, and we could use their bathroom and living-room as well if we wanted to. We were away all day, and on our return we found our bed made up, clean, and smelling fresh. Still, we didn't sleep much, because as soon as we switched off the light the bed-bugs came out for their dinner. We could hardly wait for the morning and our escape, checking in this time at a proper hotel.

A few years later, on our second visit, we noticed that life had changed in Hungary. There were lots of cars, mainly East German *Trabants*, emitting smoke, and, when they were not being driven, parked on the pavement because there was not enough space on the road. My Hungarian friend asked me: 'Do you know how to double the value of a *Trabant*?'

'No….'

'Fill it up with petrol.'

They were noisy and dirty, but still they were very

precious to their owners, enabling them to drive as far as Italy. People showed off and competed with each other by way of cars, a *Skoda* being better than the Russian *Zsiguli*, which in turn was better than the Romanian *Dacia*, with the bottom of the list being taken up by the *Trabant*. Dogs, especially exotic dogs, had become popular. I have never seen so many Afghan hounds and huge Newfoundlanders as in Budapest. There was plenty of food in the shops, and also now some industrial goods, but the quality was not what we had been used to in the West. We took with us coffee, tea, and small kitchen appliances as presents for our relatives.

We found more favouritism and corruption, though. Under the strict communist regime, ordinary people were not corrupt, mainly because there was nothing they could do with their money. Corruption was restricted to those in power, people like customs officers, who earned really big money which they could use to buy a flat. Because there was no free market in flats, this too in turn involved more corruption. Now more goods were available, and a differentiation by wealth had started. Doctors expected to be paid extra money, officials were expecting presents.... What was an ordinary shopkeeper expected to do? I wanted to buy a pair of shoes I had seen in a shop window.

'This is what I want!' I pointed at it. 'In a size 42.'

'We only have a size 40,' the saleswoman said without hesitation. I handed her some cash, perhaps one-fifth of the price of the shoes.

'Would you look in the store room? Maybe you'll find a pair.'

She took the money quite openly, but didn't go to the store room, only to the back of the shop, from where she brought out a pair of size 42s.

Visiting Hungary

I wanted to buy a four-volume book, a lexicon of the arts. I was told that it was out of print but that I might be able to find it in an antiquarian bookshop. There were several such shops in Budapest, and I went to all of them in vain, since none of them had the book in stock. In desperation, in the last shop I indicated to the uninterested manager, who was almost asleep, my willingness to pay above the official price.

'Just a minute,' he said, immediately perking up and phoning another shop I had just visited. 'Have you got that four-volume art lexicon in stock?' he asked. Someone spoke on the other end of the line. 'And what do you want in return?' he asked again. 'Yes, I have it,' he said, 'I'll reserve it for you.'

He asked for a bribe, leaving the exact amount up to me. I gave him half the official price, and we were both highly satisfied. Then I went back to the other shop, where I was already expected, and received the four books, neatly packed, at the normal price. The manager of that shop, in turn, would get his bribes from other customers who wanted books reserved for them at the first shop. Everybody was happy. Economists say that for a healthy economy money must flow, and that the black market can contribute to the national economy.

I visited a university city, Veszprém, and stayed in a nice-looking hotel. On checking in I asked for a room with a private bathroom. It was clean but very noisy, as it overlooked a busy road with lots of traffic. I went down to reception wanting to change to a room overlooking the rear. They were available, and also cheaper, but none of these rooms had private bathrooms and I didn't want to risk being obliged to use a communal one. So I negotiated.

'Is the hotel full?' I began.

'No, we've plenty of empty rooms,' said the receptionist.

'I'll take a room at the back to sleep in, but I also want

the key to a room at the front where I can use the bathroom. Of course, I'll pay the higher price for my room at the back.' It worked well, and I'm sure that the price difference was never recorded in the official register.

Antiques and old masters were much cheaper in Hungary than in the West, but exporting them was forbidden. Exporting paintings by living artists was allowed, but to tourists only and for convertible currency at the official exchange rate. We went to the *atelier* of a painter who'd been recommended to us. He was an old man with long, white hair, which was considered the trademark of a true artist. His wife and son too were both painters in their own right. He lived in a modest apartment and his studio was in his living-room. We bought a painting from him, a scene of a village market where the local peasants bought and sold their animals. It reminded me of my home village of Orosháza. We agreed on a price, and I was hoping that I could pay at the black-market exchange rate.

'The way to do this,' the painter said, 'is to pay me half the agreed price, in Dutch *guilders*, using the black-market rate, for which I won't give a receipt. Instead, I'll give you a letter saying that I sold you the painting, quoting half the agreed price, but in Hungarian *forints*. You'll then take his letter to the Art Council and pay the money in hard currency at the official exchange rate and give them your home address in Holland. This way we both benefit.'

I found this rather complicated but did as he suggested, and two weeks later the painting arrived safely in Holland by post.

We knew that it was forbidden to take Hungarian money out of the country. Returning from one of our visits to Budapest, after depositing our luggage at the airport check-in desk we proceeded to passport control but, on our

Visiting Hungary

way, we were stopped by a fat, middle-aged, high-ranking, secret-police officer. I knew he was high-ranking because of the number of golden stars on his wide, golden lapels. He looked at us casually with a metal detector in his hand, and said: 'I want to check if you have any metal objects on you.' Without waiting for permission he began, concentrating his search on my pockets and, feeling my wallet, bluntly asked me to remove it. For a moment I thought of asking him if he really had the authority to searching my wallet, but quickly decided against it. He then went through its contents, obviously looking for money. He found some *guilders* and asked: 'Why do you have Dutch currency if you have a British passport?'

'Because we live in Holland,' I answered, but now I must have looked even more suspicious.

'Why, if you live in Holland, do you have no Dutch passport?' He couldn't understand the free movement of people in Europe. Had he found any Hungarian money on us, I'm sure he would simply have pocketed it. He almost certainly had no right to carry out a search without good reason, and I still think the whole thing was just a bit of private enterprise on his behalf. What would he have done if I had challenged him? It wasn't worth us trying, as we might have missed our plane.

We asked someone who looked after some properties and regularly had to engage workmen if he ever got any kickbacks from them. 'That's what we live on,' he admitted. The saddest thing was that the police too could be bribed. We heard of two such cases. One was for a speeding offence, which was bought off for about $10. The other was for driving after drinking some alcohol, a much more serious offence that required $80. This was probably a week's wages for a policeman.

WHERE IS MY HOME?

After the revolution in Hungary, travel to other communist countries was allowed, and resorts in Romania, Czechoslovakia and Yugoslavia became popular, especially those by the seaside. By that time, more and more people owned a car, though usually one made in the communist bloc. Under 'goulash communism,' limited travel to the West was also made possible, once in every three years and with certain restrictions. You were not allowed to own foreign currency, and if you were granted a passport you were allowed to buy $150 at the official exchange rate for your entire holiday. Taking *forints* out of the country was still forbidden, but in any case they would have been useless in the West. This didn't allow people to stay in hotels, so everybody planned his or her holiday route on the basis of where they had friends who could provide them with free lodgings. People used to travel with as much food as they could squeeze into their car. In later years, when an uncle of mine visited us with his wife in Holland, we were shocked when they wanted to use their own sugar, which they had brought with them, for their coffee. What's more, they told us that they always took with them a small methanol heater as well, to make coffee in their modest hotel rooms.

Another painter, whose parents lived in the same street as we had in Orosháza and whom I had known since childhood, visited us in Holland. By now he was a famous artist in Hungary, had received the prestigious Kossuth Prize, but was not allowed to export his own work. He was a large, corpulent man, with short hair, some seven years older than me, looking more like a businessman than an artist. He came with his wife and two daughters in his own car, a red *Skoda*.

'Can you give me some warm water and a sponge?' he asked after we had greeted each other. I did so. He took a piece of cardboard with newspaper glued to its entire surface out of the boot of his car, and started to wash off the newspaper to reveal an oil painting beneath. It was in perfect condition, and when it was dry he signed it by scraping his name onto it with a nail. The painting was of three fishermen on the River Tisza.

The top reward for good work was a holiday in one of the other socialist countries. At the very top of the list was Sochi, a Russian holiday resort on the Black Sea. I knew one person, a faithful communist, who was granted a one-week holiday there. On the other hand, at the bottom of the list was a holiday in North Korea, where guests were treated as if they were soldiers. They had to be exactly on time for their meals, they were not allowed to walk about on their own without an escort, and were not allowed to look down any side-roads. They got the impression that the beautiful frontages on the main roads were only a façade, and that they had nothing but slums behind them. One anecdote had it that the Communist Party was organising a lottery. First prize was a week's holiday in North Korea. Second prize a two-week holiday in North Korea....

After leaving Shell I considered doing business with Hungary. One of our constant problems had been the long waiting time for the results of analyses. Every three or four month we had to send the backlog of samples to an independent institute, who did the work for a huge fee. Because the cost of labour was much cheaper in Hungary than in Holland, and because Hungarian analytical scientists had a good international reputation, I thought that I might be able to collect samples for chemical, physical, and toxicological tests from companies in Holland, send them to a university in Hungary, and receive the results by telex. I visited Professor P, head of the analytical faculty at the Technical University of Budapest, whom I knew from our time as students. He was very interested and agreed to do his part of the work: 'When you return home,' he said, 'send me an official request and I'll send you an official quote.'

I also needed an agent, and approached a reputable firm who was the official, local agent for other big, Western companies. They too found the idea excellent. A young man was assigned to me, and accompanied me to all official discussions. He enjoyed the lunches and dinners I treated him to, and soon let me know that he would like to receive a small computer as well. 'That's the way to do business in Hungary,' I thought. We discussed some basic figures and agreed on an hourly rate for the work which was far higher than a salary in Hungary and would have provided much-needed foreign exchange. We described some basic, common analyses and the time they would take, so as to ascertain the viability of the project. It all looked very promising.

I returned to Holland, set up a company, International Scientific Services, and registered it at the local Chamber of Commerce. I wrote to tell Professor P, but didn't receive an answer; he had entered politics, and he became a minister for a while. He was disappointed not to have received a Nobel Prize for his scientific work. I also got a letter from the agent, stating that the times I had suggested for certain analyses were too short, meaning that they would cost more to do.

'My god!' I thought. 'We haven't even got off the ground, and they've already started to put their prices up!' I would have taken on the first job free of charge, as an introductory 'taster', but now I had got scared. 'This isn't going to work,' I thought. 'I'd better stop now.' I did, and I was right.

I had a similar experience with a Hungarian software firm. I let them know that Shell's analytical department wanted a software program which they could use during the analysis of spent noble-metal catalysts such as platinum. If successful, they would want other, similar programs. What was especially attractive for me and for the Hungarian firm was that Shell didn't wish to claim exclusive rights over the software, which meant that we could have sold it to other companies as well. I thought this amounted to an offer nobody could refuse, and was prepared to give up my profit on the deal just to get the ball rolling. I met a representative of the biggest Hungarian software firm, a self-assured young man, and suggested to him that the University of Budapest analytical department could provide the analytical knowledge and asked him for a price for preparing the software. He came back asking for 120,000 *Deutschmarks*. I couldn't believe it. He said it would involve one man-year of work, and that this was the cost in the West. The average salary of a graduate in Hungary at the time was the equivalent of about 10,000 DM a year. My argument was that they shouldn't be asking for a *Western* fee but instead for how much it would cost to do the work in India, where they were skilled at programming, but they never got back to me. I stopped searching for business opportunities in Hungary.

The changeover from a planned to a market-driven economy in 1989 didn't go smoothly in Hungary. Most people, except true communists, accepted the need for such change, but they hadn't realised how much individual hardship it would mean. Privatisation was an uphill struggle, accompanied by plenty of corruption. The standard of living dropped, and the polarisation between rich and poor dramatically increased. Beggars appeared on the streets, and more and more people were sleeping at underground stations or in parks. Workers were sacked in large numbers without compensation, and casual workers such as gypsies had no work at all. Most people blamed the government for introducing the changes too rapidly, especially those concerning taxation. Others blamed the banks, who refused to give unsecured loans. Most people blamed both. The situation was made a lot worse by the collapse of the Russian and other East European economies, major customers of Hungary. Factories were desperate to get orders, but had no experience in marketing and advertising and didn't know how to negotiate with foreign buyers. Hungarians developed a reputation for being pessimistic and fond of complaining. They used to say that the current year was an average one—better than next year, but worse than last year....

In one company, whose only activity was to make printed circuits for Hungarian-made buses, they suddenly found themselves without any orders. The majority of the buses had gone to Russia, who could no longer pay for them. They took on an order from Germany, which paid an hourly rate of 10 DM. Then, suddenly, the German company discontinued the order, because, as they claimed, they could have made the same product in Portugal for 4 DM.

'And what did you do?' I asked someone at the Hungarian firm.

'What could we do? We also did it for 4 DM,' he replied.

It had never occurred to anyone to check if the claim was true or just a trick to reduce the price.

The government privatised whatever they could sell, and entrepreneurs suddenly began emerging. Because many businesses were sold for far less than their true value, millionaires were created overnight. Private shops were again allowed to open, but unfortunately many shopkeepers were lacking experience. I went to a newly opened shop selling small antiques and second-hand pieces of Hungary's famous Herend porcelain. Vera liked Herend, and I wanted to buy some for her. The owner was busy organising his stock and looked very proud to be at the forefront of the changeover to capitalism.

'How much does this cost?' I asked him, pointing to a vase bearing the 'Rothschild' bird design. He quoted a price which I found far too expensive. I could buy similar articles in the state-owned shops for less, and I told him so.

'In this shop,' he said proudly, 'I decide the price.'

'That may be,' I answered, 'but I decide whether to buy it or not.' And I walked out of that budding capitalist's shop.

With Pista and Magda

We did enjoy meeting our relatives and old friends when we returned to Hungary, and we had so many invitations that we had to say no to some of them. The standard of living had improved, and the people seemed to be happy. Frequently they asked us if we would ever want to return permanently, but our answer was always no. We especially liked to visit my uncle Pista, the artist, who personally conducted us through the art galleries of Budapest explaining all the techniques the painters used.

Pista was a member of an exquisite club for artists called *Fészek* or 'The Nest', and one New Year's Eve he entertained us there with Hungarian champagne. He was one of the few people who could afford to buy a car, even if just a second-hand *Trabant* that had previously been a police-car. Because the regulations stated that even if he could afford it he had to wait three years before buying another car, he immediately put his name down for a new one. Sure enough, three years later he bought a new car and gave the old one to his wife. But Magda had no intention of using it, and through a newspaper advertisement he swapped it for a weekend retreat, a small house with a large garden full of fruit trees by the shore of the popular Lake Velence. Just imagine—a house and garden for a dilapidated old car! But such are the relative values of objects in times of shortage.

They took us to their house for a weekend, and we enjoyed fruit freshly picked from the trees and swam in the lake. They had promised us a separate bedroom if we stayed for the night. It was indeed separate, but tiny. It had two simple, wooden beds occupied half of the room from wall to wall. We are not tall people, but Pista and Magda were even shorter than us and the beds had been made for them. The sheets and blankets were similarly tiny, and after a most uncomfortable night we were glad to get back to our hotel.

The Dutch government decided to give financial aid to the ex-communist countries of East Europe, including Hungary. The help came in the form of financing four training courses for top managers of local industries. I went to Hungary as a member of the Dutch delegation to establish their management-training needs. Our Hungarian partner

Visiting Hungary

was a budding institute for managers, led by an ex-minister. They arranged a visit to different companies, and we were supposed to talk to a cross-section of their managers. However, time always proved short simply because we always had to start in the boardroom, drinking coffee and listening to endless complaints about the economy. After that we had to participate in a tour of the facilities, and then it was time for lunch. It was always a hot, three-course meal, much more elaborate than is usual in Holland, and included copious amounts of alcohol. At the first company we visited, after lunch the managing director, a badly dressed but jovial elderly man, asked me: 'Your colleagues haven't seen Budapest yet. Why don't you take the company car and show them the sights for the afternoon?'

When I translated this, my sober Dutch partners exploded. They were already uneasy at the interminable speeches, even more at the big lunch, not to mention the alcohol. They insisted on doing the interviews we had had planned, which we now conducted until dinner and evaluated in our hotel through until ten or eleven each evening.

During the interviews I met the training manager of one of the selected companies. He was a young man, no more than thirty, and smelled of aftershave. He had a pair of glasses with thick, black rims and carried a handsome, black-leather attaché case. As soon as he sat down, he removed a writing pad which had his name printed at the top of each page. Then he uncapped his black pen and placed it on the writing pad in such a way that I could see its make—Parker. I expected it to be a pleasant discussion, given our common interests, so I asked a personal question to start with: 'What sort of training would you like to have?' His answer was astonishing.

'I don't need any training. I already know everything.'

If this was the attitude of the training manager, what could one expect from the rest? Obviously they didn't know what they needed. I quickly turned to the needs of the company.

'Does your company need financial training?' I asked.

'Sure, we'll send our financial director,' he answered

'No,' I said, 'he already knows quite a lot about finance. Send the others.'

The same applied to quality control: he didn't understand why the production manager should be trained in quality-control management.

There were excellent trainers from Holland and from England, working with simultaneous translation into Hungarian, but I was the only one who didn't need a translator. This was much appreciated and helped communication in both directions. The Hungarians already knew the theory, including the theory of managing a market-oriented economy, human management, and the rest, but they had no idea how to apply this knowledge and very much appreciated my examples from real-life situations.

The training courses were held in a beautiful, old castle, recently renovated and converted into a hotel. Everybody, both trainers and participants, stayed there on full board throughout the week. This was necessary, because providing training in Hungary had its own problems. When people had more than one job, they had no time to waste on training. They were extraordinarily undisciplined. When, later on, I participated in one-day courses, some people came in one or two hours late; others (or often the same people) left one or two hours early.

At lunchtime on the first day of a course lasting four weeks, the local administrator invited me to sit with them at a separate table. Just like Oxford, I thought, with the

Visiting Hungary

lecturers sitting at high table. I thanked her, but declined and sat amongst the participants.

The scene in Hungary was also ripe for all sort of charlatans, mainly Hungarians who were living in America. They advertised expensive seminars on behaviour and self-improvement. At one seminar they mentally tortured the participants, shouting at them, calling them by names to make them feel like dirt. The participants had to ask permission from the trainer if they wanted to go to the toilet, and permission was regularly refused. They had to wait for the break. Plenty of people took the course, but I couldn't see how it helped their self-development.

During one of the training sessions we gave I met Gyuri, who had started his own training centre in another big city. I liked his commercial attitude and his enthusiasm and agreed to help him by being his guest speaker whenever I was in Hungary; he had only to pay my local expenses. The most popular subjects I had to cover were human management, quality management, and decision making. He always filmed my courses, and I knew that he was trying to copy me and my style, but I didn't mind. I treated him almost as a son. The training was always a great success, and occasionally he took me to the local radio station to be interviewed, or to press conferences and so forth.

Gyuri was a real extrovert, proudly showing off his achievements. The walls in his office were full of certificates and diplomas, even if they had nothing to do with management, like being a member of a tennis club. He used to tell me how rich his company was, with all its audio and video equipment and computers. He quoted their purchase price as if they would last a lifetime. I warned him that he'd have to replace them every few years, but I didn't get through. He hired an office with four rooms, one for himself as managing director, two for training, and one as a library.

WHERE IS MY HOME?

'Why do you need a separate room as a library?' I asked. 'Why not use it as a third room for training? It'd come in very useful, because the training rooms are the bottleneck.' But he kept the library and even bought a full set of the *Encyclopaedia Britannica* for a huge sum, when hardly any of his staff could speak English. In the reception area he had three or four uniformed secretaries working, making coffee and looking after visitors. The reason for all this was that he used his library to show off to potential new clients, just as he did with the Land Rover he hired at great expense. He spent more time and money soliciting for new clients than he did keeping his existing ones satisfied. But this was not unique to Gyuri, and other companies in Hungary did the same. Training courses were generally organised in the most expensive hotels, like the Hilton, or in the most expensive restaurants, like Gundel. One day, someone wrote an important comment on the evaluation sheet: 'I liked the cakes with the coffee.'

There was a great mistrust between universities and training organisations. Professors were envious of the much higher salaries of the trainers and, in turn, trainers thought that the knowledge of the professors was too theoretical, and not useful. This was a university city, and on one occasion we invited members of the academic staff to a talk on the management of research. I insisted that it should be free; they didn't have to pay a penny. Just one professor turned up, and after my introduction, lasting only a couple of minutes, he got up and left without saying a word. Most likely he too thought that he already knew everything.

One day, Gyuri phoned me: 'Would you come over and train a very important group of my customers?'

'But I'm not planning to go to Hungary any time soon,' I replied.

'I understand,' he said. 'I'll reimburse your travel.'

Visiting Hungary

'I don't need any *forints*, thank you,' I objected.

'I'll pay you in dollars.'

I went and worked for him four days, after which he didn't pay me a penny, not even in *forints*. Obviously he hadn't hear the advice of Kövesi *bácsi*, my mentor in the labour camp during the war, about the importance of trust in business. When I asked a local friend of mine what I could do about Gyuri, he said: 'For $500 you can hire somebody to shoot him....' I didn't pursue the matter further, but felt very sad. I haven't worked for him since, and his action was a typical example of killing the goose that lays the golden egg.

I had to give a training course in another ex-communist country, Poland. Negotiating with the manager of the personnel department was the same as anywhere else. 'Have you ever worked with Polish people before?' she asked, after we had agreed on everything.

'Not in Poland,' I answered. 'But I did work with several Polish colleagues in England.'

'Then you must have observed that the Polish worker is different. He always complains.'

'Sure,' I thought, but didn't say. 'They bother you with all sort of problems. The manager of the personnel department wants a quiet life, the workers need attention.' In fact, the Polish workers turned out to be very industrious, keen, and motivated to learn and improve their performance. One of them told me during a break:

'We trust you because you're Hungarian.' Being Hungarian comes in useful sometimes!

'If a general doesn't believe in his soldiers, and doesn't trust them, he can never win a war,' I told the personnel manager in parting, after my job was done.

WHERE IS MY HOME?

During a visit to Hungary in September of 2002 I didn't do any training. Apparently there were by then a large number of home-grown experts, advisers, and trainers offering their services. I was invited to participate in a conference, where I noticed that many more people had mastered English and that the local speakers really did know what they were talking about. Still, at a workshop for members of a heavy-machinery firm, they talked about their future strategy, explaining that they planned to go on doing what they had been doing so far, making spare parts for railway wagons. They didn't think that the overall market was expanding, but they hoped to gain a greater market share.

'It won't be easy,' I warned them. 'Why don't you try to diversify into higher added-value products, like robots? You should use your workers' brains. If you want to continue making spare parts for railway wagons you have to automate the process. This in turn needs lots of capital and stays vulnerable to new technological developments.' Change management is difficult enough in the West, but it's even worse in Eastern Europe. The company is now bankrupt.

The University of Budapest decided to award a golden diploma to anybody who had received their diploma fifty years earlier. For some reason they also gave everybody 8,000 *forint*, worth about €35. They asked no questions about our achievements, and for all they cared, I could have spent the intervening half-century selling second-hand cars. I found the whole thing ridiculous and wrote a letter to the vice-chancellor saying that, as far as I could see, the only reason for the reward was that I was still alive. I received no answer.

In the meantime, István also received his PhD and became Professor of International Law at the University of

Visiting Hungary

István receives his PhD

Warwick, England. He specialised in human-rights issues and, not surprisingly, concentrated on Central and Eastern Europe. He started to visit Hungary because of his work, reading and translating disputes in parliament, and investigating the lives of the Roma people. He wrote several books on these subjects and gave numerous lectures in various countries. Vera and I are really proud of him. Later he bought a small apartment in Budapest, which he furnished tastefully and kept in beautiful condition. Occasionally we too stayed there for a couple of weeks. On one visit I wanted to buy some new curtains for the apartment and went to a shop which had been recommended. I took the measurements, selected the material, and made sure that the shop could also make the curtains and hang them, as the ceiling was rather high and I had no ladder. The right length was cut off, and I was asked to pay for it.

'Can I also pay now for the work it'll take to run them up?' I asked.

'You'll have to discuss that with the lady who'll be doing it,' they explained.

I had to wait half an hour until she arrived and started to do some calculations before quoting a price.

'Fine,' I said. 'Can I pay you now?'

'No, this is just an estimate. You have to pay when the work's finished and I know the exact amount.'

A week later I got a phone call to say the curtains were finished. 'Will the installer bring them with him?' I asked.

'No, you have to come to the shop and pay for them first.'

I went and paid the final price, which was almost exactly the same as the estimate, and the next day the handyman arrived with the curtains and a long ladder.

'Where are the runners?' I asked. 'I thought you'd bring everything you needed with you.'

'Oh, no, you should've bought those in the shop,' he said.

Nobody in the shop had warned me of this, but fortunately he had some in his van and hang up the curtains. Only then did I discover a large slit in the middle of one curtain. It had to be taken back to the shop and a new one made (free of charge!) and rehung. Then I had to pay the man for his work.

I also bought new kitchen furniture for the apartment and went to another shop outside the city. In the showroom I made my selection and wanted to place an order. I approached an assistant sitting in front of a computer, who made a full list of the chosen materials and printed out a nice picture of how the new kitchen would look. For this he asked 10,000 *forint* (about €40), which was to be refunded if I actually bought the furniture, which I did. He also quoted a date for the delivery and installation. Then I had to go to a small cashier's window. There sat a girl in a small room, in front of a computer. I paid the full price and, indeed, got my refund.

Visiting Hungary

'And when will you deliver and install it?' I asked.

'Just a minute,' said the girl behind the window, and she moved her chair a couple of metres to the right so she could sit in front of another computer, from which position she opened another small window next to the first. I then had to move over to the second window, where she told me the date and time of delivery, which differed from what the first assistant had said. Alas, the deliverymen were not qualified to install it, and installation had to be done a day *after* delivery, and by another team. Of course, first I had to have the old furniture removed and disposed of, because the deliverymen wouldn't do this either (were they not qualified?). I phoned the handyman who had hung the curtains, and he came and did the job. He said that he could use some of the old stuff himself, but I also paid him. Next day the new furniture arrived, and I had to pay the deliverymen in cash and then the installers, the next day, again in cash. It will take some time before Hungarian business becomes truly efficient.

As time passed, visiting Hungary felt more and more strange to us. We had got used to life in the West and found that Hungary had changed, often not for the better. Anti-Semitism and anti-Roma feeling was rampant. New words had appeared, often English ones, contorted to sound Hungarian, and with slang phrases we didn't understand. We knew the name of the prime minister, but none of the other people in office. We couldn't laugh at the jokes anymore, because we didn't know the people involved or the situations they referred to. Some people commented that our pronunciation had become 'foreign'. We did feel like foreigners.

Epilogue

TODAY Hungary is very much in the news in the West. The centre-right government of Viktor Orbán has a huge majority in parliament and is busy changing the constitution and placing its own, trusted people in all of the important positions. The West sees this as an attempt at dictatorship. At the same time, the neo-fascist Jobbik Party, the 'Movement for a Better Hungary', enjoys large support and is openly anti-Semitic and anti-Roma. People in Holland keep asking us: 'What's happening in your country?' But is it really 'our' country? Has it ever been? Is it possible to be Jewish and Hungarian at the same time? As a child I thought that it was. Now I'm sure it's not.

Religion is not an issue in tolerant, Dutch society, but I know that it only takes a spark for the ember of anti-Semitism to be reignited. I hope I shan't live to see this. We never talked about religion with our friends in the West, and most of them were surprised to learn that we were Jews when they read my book on my experiences during the Holocaust. Other Hungarians living in Holland did know. Last month, meeting one of them at a private birthday party, I asked a question:

'My son, who's a professor of international law at an English university, wrote in a book that he considered the Jews in Hungary between the two world wars to be a minority group. Do you consider us Hungarian, or a minority?'

He thought for a long time before answering, obviously looking for the words.

'Yes and no,' he said finally.

'What do you mean? Why "yes"?' I pressed him.

'You lived in Hungary, therefore you were Hungarian. Your origin doesn't matter.'

WHERE IS MY HOME?

'Then why "no"?'

He hesitated again, and I felt that he knew the answer but didn't know how to put it.

'You also made some mistakes, like Béla Kun….'

At this point he was interrupted by our host and couldn't finish the sentence. Béla Kun was Jewish, the leader of the short-lived communist regime in Hungary just after the First World War. Rákosi, the communist leader of Hungary after the Second World War, was also Jewish. Whatever anyone may think of them, they have nothing to do with me, but people generalise. Generalisation is so hard-wired in humanity; it must have been one of those evolutionary traits which helped us to survive.

People in Holland often ask us whether or not we are planning to return to Hungary permanently, now that there is democracy there. We tell them no. We are Jews, born in Hungary, with British nationality, living in the Netherlands. We speak three languages, but none of them absolutely 'correctly', because we mix-up words and expressions, using the first one that comes to mind. What are we? There's only one word for it: we are foreigners!

Where is our home? Vera will often use the expression 'I'm going home' whenever we are planning a trip to Hungary. I disagree. To me, 'home' is where you happen to live, where your bed is. I'm sure many Hungarians would conclude that being Jewish is the reason for my cosmopolitan attitude. They'd be wrong. There was no truer patriot than I was, right up to the point when they wanted to murder me. They made me what I am now. István likes the life in Budapest, and all the opportunities for culture and leisure that a capital city has to offer. He made many friends there, and eventually he moved back permanently. He has never hidden his Jewish background, and we were

Epilogue

powerless to observe how he disregarded our plans for his assimilation into English society. We tried. God only knows we tried, but we failed.

Last time we were in Budapest, we went to a famous fish restaurant where there was gypsy music. As usual, the bandleader came to our table and asked Vera which tune she would like them to play. It was easy, for she had one favourite: 'There's only one pretty girl in the world, and she is my sweetheart; God must have loved me when he gave her to me.'

It was a slow melody, and they played it for Vera with deep feeling. She wiped her eyes with her handkerchief and thought back to her childhood, when her father used to sing it to her. Even I shed a tear. I'm not as sentimental as Vera, and it wasn't the music. I was thinking of the sixty-five years we had spent together.

Naarden, February 2013

Printed in Great Britain
by Amazon.co.uk, Ltd.,
Marston Gate.